THE RIGHTS OF THE PEOPLE

Also by Walter Goodman

The Clowns of Commerce
All Honorable Men
The Committee
Black Bondage
A Percentage of the Take

THE RIGHTS OF THE PEOPLE

The Major Decisions of the Warren Court

ELAINE AND
WALTER GOODMAN

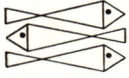

FARRAR, STRAUS AND GIROUX | NEW YORK | AN ARIEL BOOK

© 1971 by Elaine Goodman and Walter Goodman
All rights reserved
First printing, 1971
Library of Congress catalog card number: 79-157926
ISBN 0-374-36279-3
Published simultaneously in Canada
by Doubleday Canada Ltd., Toronto
Printed in the United States of America
Designed by Cynthia Basil

To some of the young people in our lives—
Bennet, Hal, Sandy, Michael, Laurie, Robin

CONTENTS

	Foreword	3
	Explanatory Note	7
	The Rights of the American People, as Guaranteed in the U.S. Constitution	9
I	Separate and Unequal	15
II	The Wall Between Church and State	39
III	The Rights of Suspected Criminals	61
IV	The Young Have Rights, Too	83
V	The Zone of Privacy	93
VI	The End of Censorship	107
VII	The Right to Be Unpopular	123
VIII	One Man—One Vote	135
IX	Milk for Children	151
	Cases Cited	163
	Justices Who Served on the Warren Court, 1953–1969	167
	Index	180

THE RIGHTS OF THE PEOPLE

FOREWORD

The "Warren Court" existed from 1953, when Earl Warren —former Governor of California and Vice Presidential candidate on the 1948 Republican Party ticket—was appointed Chief Justice by President Eisenhower, until 1969, when he resigned his high post. In a way, it is misleading to single out any period of the Supreme Court's long history and discuss it as though it stands somehow apart from the rest of that history. The Court has been operating since the beginnings of our nation; its role has developed and its views have changed as America itself has developed and changed in nearly two hundred years. It is a living body, and the Warren Court, growing out of what came before, affecting what is yet to come, can be thought of as a recent, significant chapter in that ongoing life.

The cases described here will, we hope, give readers an appreciation of what made the years between 1953 and 1969 special in the Court's history. They are cases involving the rights of the individual under the Constitution—his right to speak and publish freely, to associate with persons of his choice, to hold and advocate unpopular views without fear of harassment, to make his vote count, to receive fair treatment if he is charged with a crime, and, of course, the right not to be discriminated against on account of his race.

FOREWORD

It is these cases, taken together, that define the Warren Court.

Our courts, along with the Congress and the Presidency, make up the three separate bodies which the Founders of the nation hoped would provide checks and balances on each other and so protect the people from despotism. Their hope has been realized. The American Constitution, as interpreted and reinterpreted by the high Court, has proved to be a remarkably workable and enduring document.

By appointing our Supreme Court Justices for life, we attempt to remove them from the pressures and temptations of day-to-day politics. By holding their discussions and reaching their decisions behind closed doors, the Justices attempt to avoid the pressures of publicity. Yet even our highest court has never stood entirely above the political battle. As we shall see, the subjects with which it deals—Communism, pornography, crime, race, religion—are extremely controversial, the basic stuff of politics. The Court's rulings call forth powerful passions across the nation, and in reaching their rulings the Justices cannot escape being influenced by the temper of their times.

The Court, after all, is composed of nine human beings (seventeen Justices actually played a greater or lesser part on the Warren Court during its sixteen years), and they possess as a group all the strengths and weaknesses of humankind. The hope is, of course, that each of them will be wiser, more compassionate and dispassionate, as well as more learned, than most of his fellow citizens. But Presidents, who have the power of appointment, naturally seek to put like-minded Justices on the high bench, and so considerations other than compassion and intellect often enter into their selection. Yet men do have a way of rising to their responsibilities—and whatever one may think of any particular decision or of any particular Justice, the Supreme Court has stood over the decades as an example of how

FOREWORD

serious men, dedicated to their office, respectful of one another despite critical disagreements, can attempt to interpret to the best of their varied abilities the law of the land.

On the October day in 1953 when Earl Warren first took his place amid his new colleagues, no one could have foreseen the direction that the high Court would take in the next decade and a half. But, then, who could have foreseen the direction that the nation itself would take? The Warren Court reflected the nation's changing attitudes and styles at the same time that it influenced them. The result has been a breaking down of restrictions on what any of us may write, say, or do, along with a strengthening of the rights of the least privileged and least admired members of our society.

If the Founding Fathers returned today, they would most likely be quite surprised at the role the Supreme Court has assumed since its creation in 1789. But perhaps, reviewing the cases that we shall be reviewing here, they would find, not without satisfaction, that in recent years the Court has all in all spoken for the generous spirit of those who composed our Bill of Rights.

EXPLANATORY NOTE

In each of the cases reported here, readers will find a reference to the *majority opinion* or the *Opinion of the Court*. This opinion—written by a Justice assigned to the job by the Chief Justice or, if the Chief Justice is in the minority, by the senior member of the majority—represents the Court's decision. In addition, Justices may and frequently do write *concurring opinions* that add special thoughts of their own to the Court's ruling. If the decision is not unanimous, then one or more Justices in the minority will deliver a *dissent*. A Justice may join explicitly in the concurring or dissenting opinion of any of his colleagues, as well as in the Opinion of the Court. Although the dissenters have lost their argument in a given case, their views are nonetheless significant—for a dissent in one year can turn into a majority opinion in another.

The cases discussed in each chapter are listed as footnotes in the customary form used for easy reference. For example, the famous school-integration case is listed as *Brown* et al. *v. Board of Education of Topeka* et al., 347 U.S. 483 (1954). This means that the decision in the case, delivered in 1954, can be found on page 483 of Volume 347 of *United States Reports*, the official volumes of Supreme Court rulings. All law libraries carry a set.

THE RIGHTS OF THE AMERICAN PEOPLE, AS GUARANTEED IN THE U.S. CONSTITUTION

FIRST TEN AMENDMENTS
THE BILL OF RIGHTS (*adopted 1791*)

AMENDMENT I

Congress shall make no law respecting an establishment of religion, or prohibiting the free exercise thereof; or abridging the freedom of speech, or of the press; or the right of the people peaceably to assemble, and to petition the Government for a redress of grievances.

AMENDMENT II

A well regulated Militia, being necessary to the security of a free State, the right of the people to keep and bear Arms, shall not be infringed.

AMENDMENT III

No Soldier shall, in time of peace be quartered in any house, without the consent of the Owner, nor in time of war, but in a manner to be prescribed by law.

AMENDMENT IV

The right of the people to be secure in their persons, houses, papers, and effects, against unreasonable searches and seizures, shall not be violated, and no Warrants shall issue, but upon probable cause, supported by Oath or affirmation, and particularly describing the place to be searched, and the persons or things to be seized.

AMENDMENT V

No person shall be held to answer for a capital, or otherwise infamous crime, unless on presentment or indictment of a Grand Jury, except in cases arising in the land or naval forces, or in the Militia, when in actual service in time of War or public danger; nor shall any person be subject for the same offence to be twice put in jeopardy of life or limb; nor shall be compelled in any criminal case to be a witness against himself, nor be deprived of life, liberty, or property, without due process of law; nor shall private property be taken for public use, without just compensation.

AMENDMENT VI

In all criminal prosecutions, the accused shall enjoy the right to a speedy and public trial, by an impartial jury of the State and district wherein the crime shall have been committed, which district shall have been previously ascertained by law, and to be informed of the nature and cause of the accusation; to be confronted with the witnesses against him; to have compulsory process for obtaining witnesses in his favor, and to have the Assistance of Counsel for his defence.

RIGHTS AS GUARANTEED IN THE CONSTITUTION

AMENDMENT VII

In Suits at common law, where the value in controversy shall exceed twenty dollars, the right of trial by jury shall be preserved, and no fact tried by a jury, shall be otherwise re-examined in any Court of the United States, than according to the rules of the common law.

AMENDMENT VIII

Excessive bail shall not be required, nor excessive fines imposed, nor cruel and unusual punishment inflicted.

AMENDMENT IX

The enumeration in the Constitution, of certain rights, shall not be construed to deny or disparage others retained by the people.

AMENDMENT X

The powers not delegated to the United States by the Constitution, nor prohibited by it to the States, are reserved to the States respectively, or to the people.

In addition to the first ten Amendments, which are known as the Bill of Rights, there are several other Amendments, as well as Articles of the Constitution itself, which safeguard the individual citizen against the power of the government.

OTHER AMENDMENTS

AMENDMENT XIII (*adopted 1865*)

Sect. 1 Neither slavery nor involuntary servitude, except as a punishment for crime whereof the party shall have been duly convicted, shall exist within the United States, or any place subject to their jurisdiction.

Sect. 2 Congress shall have power to enforce this article by appropriate legislation.

AMENDMENT XIV (*adopted 1868*)

Sect. 1 All persons born or naturalized in the United States, and subject to the jurisdiction thereof, are citizens of the United States and of the State wherein they reside. No State shall make or enforce any law which shall abridge the privileges or immunities of citizens of the United States; nor shall any State deprive any person of life, liberty, or property, without due process of law; nor deny to any person within its jurisdiction the equal protection of the laws.

Sect. 5 The Congress shall have power to enforce, by appropriate legislation, the provisions of this article.

AMENDMENT XV (*adopted 1870*)

Sect. 1 The right of citizens of the United States to vote shall not be denied or abridged by the United States or by any State on account of race, color, or previous condition of servitude.

Sect. 2 The Congress shall have power to enforce this article by appropriate legislation.

AMENDMENT XIX (*adopted 1920*)

The right of citizens of the United States to vote shall not be denied or abridged by the United States or by any State on account of sex.

Congress shall have power to enforce this article by appropriate legislation.

PROVISIONS FROM THE CONSTITUTION

ARTICLE I

Sect. 9 . . . The privilege of the writ of habeas corpus shall not be suspended, unless when in cases of rebellion or invasion the public safety may require it.

No bill of attainder or ex post facto law shall be passed.

Sect. 10 No state shall . . . pass any bill of attainder, ex post facto law, or law impairing the obligation of contracts, . . .

ARTICLE III

Sect. 2 . . . The trial of all crimes, except in cases of impeachment, shall be by jury; . . .

ARTICLE IV

Sect. 2 The citizens of each state shall be entitled to all privileges and immunities of citizens in the several states.

ARTICLE VI

. . . no religious test shall ever be required as a qualification to any office or public trust under the United States.

I | SEPARATE AND UNEQUAL

> *No State shall . . . deny to any person within its jurisdiction the equal protection of the laws.*

If there is one case that has come to stand for the spirit of the Warren Court to most Americans, it is that of eight-year-old Linda Carol Brown, who, because she was black, was compelled by the regulations of her home town of Topeka, Kansas, to attend a segregated public school.

Although there was an elementary school only four blocks from where Linda and her family lived—in a white neighborhood—Linda had to go to a school twenty-one blocks from her home. This meant she had to cross a dangerous railroad bridge and wait for a crowded school bus. It also meant she had to leave the company of the children with whom she customarily played, to join children whom she did not know.

Linda's father, Oliver Brown, an assistant pastor of a

church in Topeka, joined with the parents of twelve other black children to request admission to the all-white Sumner Elementary School, which was close to their homes. "I want her to have something more to look forward to than washing dishes," said the Reverend Brown of his daughter. When they were refused admission by the principal, they went to the courts, charging that the Topeka Board of Education was denying their children "the equal protection of the laws" guaranteed by the Fourteenth Amendment to the Constitution. As one observer wrote, "Thus was born the most important case of the twentieth century."

Although the judge of the Federal District Court expressed sympathy for the children, he felt compelled to rule against them because of a decision handed down by the U.S. Supreme Court more than fifty years before. The reliance on previous decisions is basic to our judicial system. Prior rulings in related cases serve as guidelines to our judges in new cases. Without such precedents, there would be chaos. With them, our courts can operate in an orderly manner—but sometimes old rulings stand in the way of changes required by new circumstances. What seemed to make sense at one time does not necessarily make logical or moral sense fifty years later.

In passing on Linda Brown's case, the judge of the Federal District Court felt bound by the famous case of *Plessy v. Ferguson,* decided by the Supreme Court in 1896.* This dispute began on June 2, 1892, when one

* *Plessy v. Ferguson,* 163 U.S. 537 (1896).

SEPARATE AND UNEQUAL

Homer Adolph Plessy, a man who was one-eighth Negro, boarded a train in New Orleans, Louisiana, and took a vacant seat in a coach reserved for white passengers. When he refused the conductor's order to move to the coach for colored passengers, a policeman was called and Plessy was taken off the train and put into jail. He was convicted, in a New Orleans court presided over by a judge named Ferguson, of violating an 1890 Louisiana statute that required railroads to provide "separate but equal" facilities for white and colored passengers. It was one of many such laws passed by Southern states after the Reconstruction period that were designed to maintain the dominance of whites over blacks.

Carrying his appeal to the Supreme Court, Plessy argued that the law under which he had been convicted was unconstitutional because it conflicted with the Thirteenth Amendment, which abolished slavery, and the "equal protection" clause of the Fourteenth Amendment. In ruling against Plessy, the majority of the Court granted that the Fourteenth Amendment was designed "to enforce the absolute equality of the two races before the law," but emphasized that it was not designed to "abolish distinctions based upon color, or to enforce social, as distinguished from political equality, or a commingling of the two races upon terms unsatisfactory to either."

Reflecting the widely held attitudes of the period, Justice Henry B. Brown wrote:

Laws permitting, and even requiring, their separation in places where they are liable to be brought into contact does not necessarily imply the inferiority of either race to the other and have been generally, if not universally, recognized as within the competency of the state legislatures in the exercise of their police power. The most common instance of this is connected with the establishment of separate schools for white and colored children. . . .

By such reasoning, the doctrine of "separate but equal" was sanctified by the Court. But there are instances in our judicial history when a dissent rather than a majority decision is destined to become the law of the land. *Plessy v. Ferguson* was such a case. A powerful dissent, written by Justice John Marshall Harlan, exposed the "separate but equal" argument as the tool of white supremacy, which it so clearly was.

The Louisiana statute, Justice Harlan noted, was obviously designed "to exclude colored people from coaches occupied by or assigned to white persons." Under the guise of giving equal accommodation to whites and blacks, it was in fact compelling blacks to keep to themselves while traveling. This, in Justice Harlan's view, was unconstitutional: "If a white man and a black man choose to occupy the same public conveyance on a public highway, it is their right to do so, and no government, proceeding alone on grounds of race, can prevent it without infringing the personal liberty of each." In a resounding affirmation of personal liberty and civil rights, he wrote:

SEPARATE AND UNEQUAL

... In view of the Constitution, in the eye of the law, there is in this country no superior, dominant, ruling class of citizens. There is no caste here. Our Constitution is color-blind, and neither knows nor tolerates classes among citizens. In respect of civil rights, all citizens are equal before the law. The humblest is the peer of the most powerful. The law regards man as man, and takes no account of his surroundings or of his color when his civil rights as guaranteed by the supreme law of the land are involved.

It is tempting to speculate on how differently the events of recent decades might have turned out if the majority of the Court had at that time adopted Justice Harlan's reasoning. But in fact it did not—though he prophesied that one day it would—and so, nearly a half century later, when Linda Brown sought admission to a school near her home, she was blocked by the "separate but equal" doctrine.

In 1952 the *Brown* case reached the Supreme Court (on which the grandson of John Marshall Harlan was now seated), where it was grouped with similar school-segregation cases brought in behalf of a seventeen-year-old girl from Prince Edward County, Virginia, and another from Wilmington, Delaware; a thirteen-year-old boy from Clarendon, South Carolina; and a fifteen-year-old boy from the District of Columbia.* The main attorney for the black students was Thurgood Marshall, then counsel for the National Association for the Advancement of Colored People (NAACP), which had

* *Brown v. Board of Education,* 347 U.S. 483 (1954).

for years taken the lead in fighting segregation in the courts. In 1967 Marshall would be appointed to the high bench before which he argued so successfully in 1954.

The Supreme Court agreed to consider the cases grouped under *Brown v. Board of Education* and heard arguments on them shortly before Earl Warren was named Chief Justice by President Eisenhower. One novel argument offered by the NAACP was a brief statement signed by thirty-two sociologists, anthropologists, psychologists, and psychiatrists to the effect that segregation has adverse effects on both white and Negro children and that desegregation would lead to friendlier relations between the races. Never before had the opinions of social scientists been used as a major justification for a legal decision.

Earl Warren had been Chief Justice for less than a year when he wrote, in behalf of a unanimous Court, the memorable decision in the case. Justice Warren pointed out that education in America in 1954 was very much different and very much more important to a child's future success than it was in 1896, when public schooling in most places was rudimentary. "In these days," he wrote, "it is doubtful that any child may reasonably be expected to succeed in life if he is denied the opportunity of an education. Such an opportunity, where the state has undertaken to provide it, is a right which must be made available to all on equal terms."

Having set down this fundamental observation, the Chief Justice then asked the question on which the

Brown case turned: "Does segregation of children in public schools solely on the basis of race, even though the physical facilities and other 'tangible' factors may be equal, deprive the children of the minority group of equal educational opportunities?" The issue, then, was not whether the school for black children to which Linda Brown had been ordered was any worse equipped or worse run than the school for white children from which she was barred (as, in fact, Negro schools were throughout the South). Even if the two schools were found to be equal in all respects, did the very fact of the forced segregation constitute an injury to the black children?

Relying heavily on evidence from the social scientists, the Court answered that indeed it did. Justice Warren wrote:

To separate them [black children] from others of similar age and qualifications solely because of their race generates a feeling of inferiority as to their status in the community that may affect their hearts and minds in a way unlikely ever to be undone. . . . We conclude that in the field of public education the doctrine of "separate but equal" has no place. Separate educational facilities are inherently unequal.

So the ruling had been made—segregated schools stood in violation of the Constitution—but the struggle to enforce the ruling, to do away with the separate schools, was only beginning. In anticipation of the difficulties of enforcement, the Court put off for a year giving further directions as to the "when" and the "how"

of desegregation to the states and to the lower courts that would oversee the process. Then, in May 1955, it called for "a prompt and reasonable start" to school desegregation and laid down the formula that segregation must be ended "with all deliberate speed." Just what this would mean, the Court acknowledged, would vary according to the particular problems facing individual school districts—but every district was expected to demonstrate its good faith.

A number of states, including Kansas, where Linda Brown had been forced to make her long trip to school each day, complied promptly, and the forced division of its schools into white and black was ended. In border states, such as Delaware, Kentucky, Maryland, Missouri, and Oklahoma, there was little trouble. But throughout the Deep South there was resistance.

Moderate Southern opinion welcomed the Court's decision. The *Atlanta Constitution* wrote: "The Court's decision, disappointing though it is to the extremist, was the best possible decision. It recognizes the great scope and the intricate complexity of the problem. And it disappoints most of all the 'hate' groups who hoped for a decision that would produce violence." However, the moderates did not necessarily speak for the majority, nor did they occupy the seats of power.

Declared Georgia's Governor Herman Talmadge: "I do not believe in Negroes and whites associating with each other socially or in our school systems, and, as long as I am Governor, it won't happen."

In the Congress, 101 Senators and Representatives

from 11 Southern states issued a "Southern Manifesto," which labeled the *Brown* decision "a clear abuse of judicial power." The Congressmen charged that the Court was usurping the power of the separate states over their educational systems; it was attempting to make new laws despite the fact that the power to legislate was vested by the Constitution in Congress. In the angry view of the Southern Congressmen, the Court was substituting its own "personal, political, and social ideas for the established law of the land." Dozens of bills were put forward in an effort to undo the Court's decision and to slow down integration.

This was by no means the first time in the Court's history that it had been accused of attempting to legislate morality. The Court's supporters have replied that any judicial decision is to some extent a regulation of morality and that this is as it must and should be. The immediate question that faced the Court—and the nation—in the school-segregation cases was whether the determined resistance of white officials in Southern states could be overcome.

Southern resistance took various forms. There was intimidation of both white and black parents by segregationists. Delaying tactics were common. In several places the public schools were simply shut down and public funds were channeled into "private" schools for white children. In other places segregationists resorted to violence. More than one hundred pieces of legislation aimed at keeping schools segregated were passed in the Southern states. Since the high Court has no policing powers, it was up to the lower courts to deal with persons who defied the desegregation ruling. They could be held in contempt of court if they violated a court order, and be threatened with fines or imprisonment.

The most dramatic encounter between the power of the federal government and that of a state came in Little Rock, Arkansas. Just three days after the *Brown* decision, the Little Rock District School Board publicly stated its intention to comply with the new federal requirements and set to work studying the problems involved in making the transition to a desegregated public-school system. A plan was developed whereby desegregation of the city's high schools would begin in the fall of 1957 and continue in stages until, by 1963, white and black students would be going to school together on every grade level. At the very time that this planning was going on, however, an amendment to the state constitution was adopted that commanded the Arkansas General Assembly to oppose desegregation.

In accord with the school-board program, nine black children were scheduled for admission to the city's high school in September 1957. One day before the beginning of classes, Governor Orval E. Faubus sent units of the state National Guard to the high school—which he placed "off limits" to black students. This was done without consultation with school authorities. When the nine students attempted to walk into the high school, they were blocked by guardsmen. As Justice Felix

Frankfurter would later observe, state power was being used not to uphold the law but to thwart it.

After three weeks of such obstruction, a federal district court ordered the Governor and National Guard officers to desist. The National Guard was withdrawn, and on Monday, September 23, the black students entered the school under the protection of local police. But by then community passions had been aroused; a large, potentially violent crowd had gathered, and the children had to be escorted from the school for their own protection.

Two days later, President Eisenhower ordered a thousand paratroopers into Little Rock—the first time since Reconstruction days that troops had been sent into the South to protect the rights of black people. The National Guard was federalized, and in November guardsmen took over the patrol of Central High from the paratroopers—this time to make sure that no one interfered with the black children's school attendance for the remainder of the term.

In February 1958 the Little Rock District School Board and the Superintendent of Schools went into federal district court seeking permission to postpone their program for desegregation for two and a half years; the black students already in Central High would be withdrawn. The reasons given for the request included the "chaos, bedlam, and turmoil" at Central High; "repeated incidents of more or less serious violations directed against the Negro students and their property";

"tension and unrest among the school administrators, the classroom teachers, the pupils and the latter's parents"; a "serious financial burden" to the School District; and a continuing need for a military guard—adding up to "intolerable" conditions for education.

The school board laid the blame for this unhappy condition squarely on state officials:

> The legislative, executive, and judicial departments of the state government opposed the desegregation of Little Rock schools by enacting laws, calling out troops, making statements vilifying federal law and federal courts, and failing to utilize state law-enforcement agencies and judicial processes to maintain public peace.

The District Court granted the school board the relief it requested, but was overruled by the Court of Appeals, and the case went to the Supreme Court.*

The high Court expressed sympathy for the predicament of the school board—caught as it was between a federal command to integrate its schools and state pressures to prevent desegregation. But, as a legal scholar has observed, this case represented "a challenge by a state to federal authority, the United States Constitution, and the rule of law," and the justices could not let it pass. In Justice Frankfurter's view, given in a strong concurring opinion in the case, for the Constitution to bow to the force of the state would be "to enthrone official lawlessness." He warned that violent resistance to the law by persons in authority was "profoundly subversive"

---

* *Cooper v. Aaron,* 358 U.S. 1 (1958).

both of our constitutional system and of a democratic society.

A day after hearing the arguments, the Court declared unanimously that the desegregation process must be continued—saving its statement of views until later. The decision went directly to the point:

> The constitutional rights of respondents [the black students] are not to be sacrificed or yielded to the violence and disorder which have followed upon the actions of the Governor and the Legislature . . . law and order are not here to be preserved by depriving the Negro children of their constitutional rights. . . . In short, the constitutional rights of children not to be discriminated against in school admission on grounds of race or color declared by this Court in the *Brown* case can neither be nullified openly and directly by state legislators or state executive or judicial officers, nor nullified indirectly by them through evasive schemes for segregation whether attempted "ingeniously or ingenuously."

Ordinarily, a Court opinion is attributed to a single Justice, but in this case, to draw attention to the significance of the decision and to emphasize the Court's solidarity, the opinion was signed by every Justice, three of whom had been appointed to the Court after the *Brown* decision. The Justices were entirely agreed that:

> The principles announced in that decision and the obedience of the States to them, according to the command of the Constitution, are indispensable for the protection of the freedoms guaranteed by our fundamental charter for all of us. Our constitutional ideal justice under law is thus made a living truth.

With words such as these, the Court left no doubt of its determination to enforce its ruling that schools may not be segregated by law. But enforcement turned out to be extremely difficult. In 1964, ten years after the *Brown* decision, only 10 per cent of the black students in the South were attending integrated schools.

One of the original cases decided in 1954 involved Prince Edward County in Virginia. Nearly half of the thirty thousand residents of this rural area about sixty miles southwest of Richmond were black. Instead of beginning to integrate their schools in the fall of 1959, as ordered by the courts, county officials simply closed down the public-school system. They were abetted in this by the Virginia state legislature, which had earlier passed a statute (later ruled invalid) shutting down any public school where whites and Negroes were enrolled together; then, in 1959, it repealed the state's compulsory school-attendance law and initiated a "freedom of choice" program. Private schools for white children were set up in the county—with the financial support of county and state—but no provision was made for the county's seventeen hundred black children, who remained without schooling for four years. A district court noted that the end result of every action taken by the County Board of Supervisors "was designed to preserve the separation of the races in the schools of Prince Edward County." President Kennedy was moved to remark in 1963 that there were only four places in the world where children did not have the right to attend school—North Vietnam, North Korea, Cambodia, and Prince Edward County!

At length, in 1964, the Prince Edward County case reached the Supreme Court, and once again the Justices ruled unanimously that the county's actions were unconstitutional.* Delivering the Court's opinion, Justice Hugo L. Black, himself a native Southerner, cut sharply through the web of explanations offered by county officials. "Prince Edward's public schools," he ruled, "were closed and private schools operated in their place with state and county assistance, for one reason, and one reason only: to ensure, through measures taken by the county and the State, that white and colored children in Prince Edward County would not, under any circumstances, go to the same school." Observing that "there has been entirely too much deliberation and not enough speed" in enforcing the children's consitutional rights, Justice Black concluded:

The time for mere "deliberate speed" has run out, and that phrase can no longer justify denying these Prince Edward County school children their constitutional rights to an education equal to that afforded by the public schools in other parts of Virginia.

Despite the Court's ringing reaffirmations of its ruling against segregated schools, segregation continues to be a fact of school life through much of the Deep South. (In Northern cities, too, there are predominantly black schools and predominantly white schools—but this is

* *Griffin v. County School Board of Prince Edward County,* 377 U.S. 218 (1964).

due mainly to neighborhood residential patterns rather than to laws forbidding black and white children from attending classes together.) Throughout the 1960's and into the 1970's, new cases continued to be brought before the courts. Whether and when integration will in fact be carried out now depends less on the Supreme Court—which has the power to interpret the law but not to enforce it—than on the determination and effectiveness of the U.S. Department of Justice in bringing suits to compel compliance with the law. Today, in the second decade since the *Brown* decision, the bleak fact is that most black children in the South still do not attend schools with white children.

Despite the continuing resistance to integrated schools, the *Brown* decision remains a momentous one. The Court's reasoning was applied to the opening up of public facilities of all sorts to black citizens, and it drew public attention and concern to the disadvantages under which black people in this country had labored since the Emancipation. The decision was instrumental in bringing on the great civil-rights upsurge of the early 1960's, culminating in the Civil Rights Act of 1964, whose provisions the Court has upheld.

The most controversial section of this wide-ranging law, prohibited discrimination in such public places as restaurants, movie theaters, and hotels:

All persons shall be entitled to full and equal enjoyment of the goods, services, facilities, privileges, advantages, and accommodations of any place of public accommodations

... without discrimination or segregation on the ground of race, color, religion, or national origin.

This section was challenged by an Alabama motel-owner, who refused to rent any of his 216 rooms to black travelers. The Court decided that since the Constitution gave Congress the power to regulate interstate commerce and since the motel in question served mainly travelers from other states, the owner had to abide by the Civil Rights Act.*

In his ruling, Justice Tom C. Clark reviewed the testimony heard by Congress when the law was being drawn up, pointing out:

... that our people have become increasingly mobile, with millions of all races traveling from State to State: that Negroes in particular have been the subject of discrimination in transient accommodations, having to travel great distances to secure the same; that often they have been unable to obtain accommodations and have had to call upon friends to put them up overnight; and that these conditions had become so acute as to require the listing of available lodgings for Negroes in special guidebooks, which was itself dramatic testimony of the difficulties Negroes encounter in travel. These exclusionary practices were found to be nationwide. . . .

Justice William O. Douglas wrote a concurring opinion, in which he argued that the Fourteenth Amendment could be interpreted to bar such discrimination even if it were not done in interstate commerce. Had the Court so ruled, he wrote, that would have resulted in "putting an end to all obstructionist strategies and allowing every

* *Heart of Atlanta Motel v. United States,* 379 U.S. 241 (1964).

person—whatever his race, creed, or color—to patronize all places of public accommodation without discrimination whether he travels interstate or intrastate."

In 1967 the Court struck down a particularly obnoxious sort of racial discrimination when it overturned a Virginia ban on interracial marriage—a popular law through Southern and border states. The case focused on a black woman and a white man who had been married in Virginia in 1958. They were arrested there and given a sentence of one year in jail. The trial judge told them:

Almighty God created the races white, black, yellow, malay, and red, and he placed them on separate continents. And but for the interference with His arrangement, there would be no cause for such marriages. The fact that He separated the races shows that He did not intend for the races to mix.

The judge suspended the sentences on condition that the couple, appropriately named Loving, leave the state. This they did, but returned to Virginia five years later to visit the wife's parents. They were again arrested, and the state's Supreme Court of Appeals upheld their conviction and the statute against mixed marriages.

This ruling was overturned by the Supreme Court, in a decision written by Chief Justice Warren.* He emphasized:

The Fourteenth Amendment requires that the freedom of choice to marry not be restricted by invidious racial dis-

* *Richard Perry Loving* et ux. *v. Virginia*, 388 U.S. 1 (1967).

criminations. Under our Constitution, the freedom to marry, or not to marry, a person of another race resides with the individual and cannot be infringed by the State. These convictions must be reversed.

Another popular Southern statute declared unconstitutional by the Court was the poll tax.* In outlawing the imposition of a small fee on voters in Virginia as a violation of the "Equal Protection Clause" of the Fourteenth Amendment, the majority of the Court ruled, in Justice Douglas's words: ". . . wealth or fee-paying has, in our view, no relation to voting qualifications; the right to vote is too precious, too fundamental, to be so burdened or conditioned."

Was the Court "making new law," as charged, when it reversed its nineteenth-century ruling of *Plessy v. Ferguson,* as well as other previous rulings that had upheld poll taxes and state bans on interracial sexual relations and permitted discrimination in public accommodations? No doubt the law was being changed—and drastically. Yet it is just this kind of reinterpretation of the law, on occasion necessitating a reversal of its own rulings, that gives the Court its special importance as the custodian of the Constitution. In 1896 the Court might argue that "legislation is powerless to eradicate racial instincts or to abolish distinctions based upon physical differences. . . ." By 1954 most educated Americans doubted the existence of "racial instincts" and had concluded that legislation was essential if the rights of

* *Harper v. Virginia Board of Elections,* 383 U.S. 663 (1966).

the nation's black people were to be protected and advanced. If the Constitution is to remain a potent document, then it must be read and reread in the light of the innumerable changes that have taken place in America since it was written—and that continue to take place. Such was the philosophy-in-action of the Warren Court.

Of the five youths in whose names *Brown v. Board of Education* was argued, only Linda Brown ever actually got to attend a nonsegregated school. In the past two decades new opportunities have been opened to black Americans and an impressive number have at last begun to partake of the benefits of the society that have for so long been denied them. Yet today many black people, in the North as well as in the South, still are trapped in ghettos. The Warren Court did what it could to confirm the American principle of equality before the law. It remains for other branches of the government and for the nation as a whole to see to it that the principles so eloquently laid down by the Court are turned into reality.

	Brown v. Board of Education 1954	Cooper v. Aaron 1958	Griffin v. County School Board 1964
BLACK	Concurred	OPINION OF COURT	OPINION OF COURT
REED	Concurred		
FRANKFURTER	Concurred	OPINION OF COURT	
DOUGLAS	Concurred	OPINION OF COURT	Concurred
JACKSON	Concurred		
BURTON	Concurred	OPINION OF COURT	
CLARK	Concurred	OPINION OF COURT	Concurred, but disagreed in part
MINTON	Concurred		
WARREN	OPINION OF COURT	OPINION OF COURT	Concurred
HARLAN		OPINION OF COURT	Concurred, but disagreed in part
BRENNAN		OPINION OF COURT	Concurred
WHITTAKER		OPINION OF COURT	
STEWART			Concurred
WHITE			Concurred
GOLDBERG			Concurred
FORTAS			
MARSHALL			

Heart of Atlanta Motel v. U.S. 1964	Loving v. Virginia 1967	Harper v. Board of Elections 1966
Concurring opinion	Concurred	Dissenting opinion
Concurring opinion	Concurred	OPINION OF COURT
OPINION OF COURT	Concurred	Concurred
Concurred	OPINION OF COURT	Concurred
Concurred	Concurred	Dissenting opinion
Concurred	Concurred	Concurred
Concurred	Concurring opinion	Dissented (joined Harlan)
Concurred	Concurred	Concurred
Concurring opinion		
	Concurred	Concurred

II | THE WALL BETWEEN CHURCH AND STATE

Congress shall make no law respecting an establishment of religion. . . .

The opening words of our Bill of Rights are these: "Congress shall make no law respecting an establishment of religion, or prohibiting the free exercise thereof . . ." In this way, the Founding Fathers, descendants of men and women who had fled the Old World in search of religious freedom, put into force their conviction that every American should be permitted to worship according to his own beliefs, without interference from the government.

The history of religious oppression and discrimination throughout the world is a long and bitter one. Even after coming to these shores, groups that had been discriminated against by the Church of England, which was supported by the British government, attempted to make their own churches the official religious bodies of the colonies where they settled. The opening clause of the First Amendment, the Establishment Clause, clearly forbade the creation of such officially sanctioned churches.

The author of the First Amendment, James Madison, warned forcefully of the need to be alert to even minor or indirect infringements of religious liberty. He asked:

> Who does not see that the same authority which can establish Christianity, in exclusion of all other Religions, may establish with the same ease any particular sect of Christians, in exclusion of all other sects? That the same authority which can force a citizen to contribute three pence only of his property for the support of any one establishment, may force him to conform to any other establishment in all cases whatsoever?

Justice Black would write, nearly two centuries later, that the Establishment Clause rested on "the belief that a union of government and religion tends to destroy government and degrade religion" and on "an awareness of the historical fact that governmentally established religions and religious persecutions go hand in hand." In Justice Black's words:

> The history of governmentally established religion, both in England and in this country, showed that whenever government had allied itself with one particular form of religion, the inevitable result had been that it had incurred the hatred, disrespect, and even contempt of those who held contrary beliefs.

The First Amendment's prohibition was effective. There has never been an officially established church in this country, and Americans have been free to worship in their own diverse ways. Nevertheless, the interpretation of the Establishment Clause has remained one of the most delicate issues facing our courts. Most Americans do profess a belief in God and membership in some organized religious body, usually a Christian church. The courts have had the task of drawing and redrawing the line of separation between church and state.

How far may the federal government or a state government go in cooperating with religious groups without infringing on the First Amendment? In a nation like ours, at what point does official recognition of the beliefs of a majority impinge on the rights of minorities? The difficulty of such questions became evident in two cases that focused on the connection between religion and the public schools, which were decided before Justice Warren took his place on the high bench.

In the 1940's many school systems around the country operated "released-time" programs, under which students could be released from regular classes for a period of religious instruction in their particular faith. In the schools of Champaign, Illinois, for example, the religious instruction was given in the classrooms and the teachers of religion, though not paid by the public schools, were under the supervision of school authorities. Children who did not wish to participate were sent to other classrooms while the religious instruction was under way.

Considering this situation in 1948, the Court found

that it violated the First Amendment (which had been applied to the states by the Fourteenth Amendment).* Holding to the principle that a "high and impregnable wall" must be maintained between church and state, Justice Black ruled that the use of tax-supported property, such as the public schools, for purposes of religious instruction was unconstitutional.

This decision roused a great furor around the country, with critics charging that it was an assault on religious worship. A few years later, in 1952, the Court was confronted with another "released-time" case—this one in New York.† It differed from the Illinois case in that students were permitted to leave their schools at specified times for religious instruction elsewhere, at the written request of their parents.

This type of released-time system was upheld by a divided Court. Writing for the majority, Justice Douglas pointed out that whereas in the Illinois case classrooms had been turned over to religious instructors, under the New York arrangement, "no one is forced to go to the religious classroom and no religious exercise or instruction is brought to the classrooms of the public schools. A student need not take religious instruction. He is left to his own desires as to the manner or time of his religious devotions, if any."

In his decision, Justice Douglas attempted to reconcile the First Amendment's absolute prohibition of any established religion with the prevailing religious beliefs

* *McCollum v. Board of Education,* 333 U.S. 203 (1948).
† *Zorach v. Clauson,* 343 U.S. 306 (1952).

of the nation. He pointed out that cooperation between official bodies and religious groups in America takes many forms that are not outlawed by the First Amendment:

We are a religious people whose institutions presuppose a Supreme Being. We guarantee the freedom to worship as one chooses. We make room for as wide a variety of beliefs and creeds as the spiritual needs of man deem necessary. We sponsor an attitude on the part of government that shows no partiality to any one group and that lets each flourish according to the zeal of its adherents and the appeal of its dogma. When the State encourages religious instruction or cooperates with religious authorities by adjusting the schedule of public events to sectarian needs, it follows the best of our traditions. For it then respects the religious nature of our people and accommodates the public service to their spiritual needs.

Justices Black, Jackson, and Frankfurter disagreed. In a sharply worded dissent, Justice Black wrote that in his view the New York released-time arrangement was unconstitutional even though the religious instruction was given outside the classroom, because the state was using its powers for the benefit of religious sects: "New York is manipulating its compulsory education law to help religious sects get pupils. This is not separation but combination of Church and State." He went on: "State help to religion injects political and party prejudice into a holy field. It too often substitutes force for prayer, hate for love, and persecution for persuasion. Government should not be allowed, under cover of the soft euphemism of 'cooperation,' to steal into the sacred area of religious choice. . . ."

In a separate dissent, Justice Robert H. Jackson, whose own children had attended privately supported church schools, objected vigorously to the New York released-time law on the grounds that it was a way of using the state to force children to go to Church schools. He referred to "the truant officer who, if the youngster fails to go to the Church school, dogs him back to the public schoolroom," which then serves as "a temporary jail for a pupil who will not go to Church." And he charged that the wall between church and state was being "warped and twisted" by the decision in this case.

A few months before the second released-time decision was handed down, another controversy involving religion and the public schools was just getting under way. In November 1951 the New York State Board of Regents, which oversees New York's school system, drew up a short nonsectarian prayer that it recommended for daily recitation by pupils in the state's schools: "Almighty God, we acknowledge our dependence upon Thee, and we beg Thy blessings upon us, our parents, our teachers, and our Country." No school was compelled to adopt the regents' prayer—which seemed bland and inoffensive to most people—and as it turned out, only a small percentage of schools did adopt it.

One of these was the school board of New Hyde Park, New York. The board notified parents in 1958 that their children would henceforward be expected to say the prayer aloud, in the presence of a teacher, at the beginning of each school day. New Hyde Park, a Long Island suburb of New York City, has a substantial Jewish population. Having had a history of long-suffering oppression by many rulers in many lands because of their religion, Jewish Americans tend to be especially sensitive to their minority status and especially resistant to any move by any government to impinge on the religious life of its citizens. As one resident of New Hyde Park, a businessman named Lawrence Roth, put it, "We believe religious training is the prerogative of the parent . . . and not the duty of the government."

Mr. Roth, who had two children in the community's schools, sought help from the New York branch of the American Civil Liberties Union, an organization dedicated to the defense of the Bill of Rights. Roth, who, though nominally Jewish, belonged to no organized religious body, placed advertisements in a local newspaper, asking other troubled parents to join him in a suit against the school board. He found about fifty people who agreed with him, but only five actually joined in the court action that began in 1959. One sympathetic parent said, "It's foolish to get mixed up in all unpopular causes."

The complaining parents felt that the school prayer "was contrary to the beliefs, religions, and religious practices of both themselves and their children," and so violated both the First and the Fourteenth Amendments. They lost their case in the lower courts; the New York Court of Appeals held that as long as no student was compelled to recite the prayer, it did not violate the constitutional guarantee of freedom of religion. And so the case went to the Supreme Court.* Stephen Engel, whose name was used to identify the case, was one of the complaining parents. William J. Vitale, Jr., the respondent, was presiding officer of the New Hyde Park School Board.

As frequently happens in cases that involve matters of principle directly affecting large numbers of people, both sides—petitioners and respondents—were joined by outside groups having a special interest in the issue. They offered arguments as *amici curiae,* friends of the court. On the side of the parents, urging the Supreme Court to reverse the lower courts' ruling, were the American Ethical Union, the American Jewish Committee, and the Synagogue Council of America. On the side of the school board were the attorneys general of twenty-two states that had provisions for school prayer.

The Warren Court handed down its decision in 1962. With the single dissent of Justice Potter Stewart, the Court agreed with the petitioning parents that the use of the regents' prayer in the public schools breached the wall of separation between church and state that had been set up by the Constitution. To Justice Black, the Establishment Clause of the First Amendment meant that "in this country it is no part of the business of government to compose official prayers for any group of the American people to recite as a part of a religion program carried on by government."

* *Engel v. Vitale,* 370 U.S. 421 (1962).

THE WALL BETWEEN CHURCH AND STATE

Justice Black emphasized the place of the First Amendment in American history:

> The First Amendment was added to the Constitution to stand as a guaranty that neither the power nor the prestige of the Federal Government would be used to control, support, or influence the kinds of prayer the American people can say—that the people's religions must not be subjected to the pressures of government for change each time a new political administration is elected to office . . . government in this country, be it state or federal, is without power to prescribe by law any particular form of prayer which is to be used as an official prayer in carrying on any program of governmentally sponsored religious activity.

In his dissent, Justice Stewart, an Episcopalian, argued that the majority was misapplying the Establishment Clause of the First Amendment:

> I cannot see how an "official religion" is established by letting those who want to say a prayer say it. On the contrary, I think that to deny the wishes of these school children to join in reciting this prayer is to deny them the opportunity of sharing in the spiritual heritage of our Nation.

But Justice Douglas, in a forceful concurring opinion, held that the Constitution permitted no government support for religion in any form, however innocuous. "Once government finances a religious exercise," he warned, "it inserts a divisive influence into our communities."

The criticisms of the Court aroused by this school-prayer decision exceeded even those aroused by the school-integration decision of 1954. The Roman Catholic hierarchy in this country was unanimous in its opposition: United States cardinals called it "shocking," "scandalizing," "fuel for Communist propaganda." The support of the Catholic Church for school prayer in 1962 was very different from the attitudes of new Catholic immigrants a century earlier, who had refused to allow their children to participate in religious exercises because they tended to be Protestant in nature. In 1840 devout Catholics rioted in New York to protest the use of the Protestant King James Bible in the public schools. But by 1962 Catholic spokesmen were in the forefront of those who demanded school prayer. The independent Catholic magazine *America* called the Court ruling "quite literally a stupid decision, a doctrinaire decision, a decision that spits in the face of our history, our tradition, and our heritage as a religious people." A bishop in Texas said, "American public schools will have to start bootlegging religion into the classroom."

Some Protestant leaders, too, were critical of the Court. "It's like taking a star or stripe off the flag," said a Methodist bishop. Declared Billy Graham, the famous evangelist, "The framers of the Constitution meant we were to have freedom of religion—not freedom from religion." Eminent figures, including former Presidents Dwight Eisenhower and Herbert Hoover, added their voices to those of the critics. But President John F. Kennedy pointed out at a press conference that the Court had not made prayer illegal—only a specific religious act in a specific place.

The Catholic President, backed by leaders of many Protestant denominations, suggested that the decision might "be a welcome reminder to every American family that we can pray a good deal more at home, that we can attend our churches with a good deal more fidelity. . . . I would hope that all of us will support the Constitution and the responsibility of the Supreme Court in interpreting it."

Newspaper editorials were severely critical, undoubtedly reflecting the views of most readers. A Gallup poll taken at about this time showed that 79 per cent of the nation favored religious observance in the schools. "How can we be so blind and naïve as to sacrifice a prayer like this," asked a Chicago man, "in order to appease a few agnostics and atheists?" School officials in a number of states avowed their intention to continue having prayers read in their classrooms no matter what the Court ruled: "A school without a prayer is not a school," stated a group of school superintendents in Long Island. Opponents of the decision even put out a record for children:

>Poor little prayer
>Poor little prayer
>My, but you stirred up a fuss.
>Meetings were held
>And you were expelled
>And taken away from us.

On the other hand, the National Council of Churches, the country's largest Protestant group, declared, "Neither true religion nor good education is dependent upon the devotional use of the Bible in the public-school program."

In Congress, the most vehement denunciations of the decision came from Southerners, who had not forgiven the Court for its ruling on school desegregation. The Justices, charged a Representative from Alabama, had "put the Negroes in the schools and now they've driven God out." A Mississippi Democrat called the decision part of a "deliberate and carefully planned conspiracy to substitute materialism for spiritual values." A New York Republican held it to be "the most tragic decision in the history of the United States." In the House of Representatives 147 bills were put forward, and in the Senate, 30, to undo the Court's decision.

A proposed amendment to the Constitution to permit prayers in the schools was supported by almost all the nation's governors. It stated: "Nothing in this Constitution shall be deemed to prohibit the offering, reading from, or listening to prayers or biblical Scriptures, if participation therein is on a voluntary basis, in any governmental or public school, institution, or place." However, constitutional amendments, though easy enough to propose, are difficult to translate into law. They must be approved by two-thirds of the House and Senate and then ratified by at least thirty-eight of the fifty states. Despite the furor, the proposed school-prayer amendment fizzled.

The Roth family, meanwhile, was receiving its own barrage of criticism, not all of it well-mannered. "You Communist kike," said one anonymous caller, "why don't you go back to Russia?" Reacting to the more vicious calls, Mrs. Roth commented, "If their God teaches them to wish my kids get polio and my house be bombed, then I think He hasn't done a very good job with them."

The commotion over the released-time decisions had not yet died down when the Court agreed to hear two other cases having to do with religion in the public schools. One came from a town near Philadelphia. A Pennsylvania state law required that "at least ten verses from the Holy Bible shall be read, without comments, at the opening of each public school on each day." In the schools of Abington Township, it was the custom, after the Bible was read over the public-address system, for students to stand and recite the Lord's Prayer.

One of the students who found himself participating in these services from 8:15 to 8:30 each morning in the 1956–57 school year was a junior named Ellory Schempp. Ellory's family were Unitarians, a group that stresses freedom of religious belief. Ellory asked to be excused from the morning exercises, and then, with the help of the American Civil Liberties Union, the Schempps brought suit against the school board to end the daily Bible readings on the grounds that they violated the Establishment Clause of the First Amendment. Ellory and his younger brother and sister, also students in Abington Township, became celebrities: some of their friends wanted to know more about their family's beliefs; others simply called them "Bible-haters."

The Schempp case came before a three-judge Federal District Court in Pennsylvania which found the practice of reading Bible passages in schools and having students recite the Lord's Prayer unconstitutional. By using the New Testament, observed the judges, the state was showing a preference for the Christian religion, and by reading the Bible passages without comment, it was acting contrary to the belief of Unitarians, who do not accept a literal interpretation of the Bible.

Before the school board's appeal reached the Supreme Court, the Pennsylvania state legislature amended the law to permit students to be excused from religious exercises if a parent so desired. In practice, this meant that the excused students would have to leave their classrooms and stand in the hall, as though they were being disciplined. The case was returned to the three-judge court, which noted that compulsion on a boy or girl to do whatever most other students do "may be subtle and thus particularly effective in respect to children." The court reaffirmed its decision that the Bible-reading law, even in its more flexible form, was in violation of the First Amendment.

At about the same time, a similar case was making its way up to the Supreme Court from Baltimore, Maryland, where the school day was opened by a reading from the New Testament and/or the Lord's Prayer. An eighth-grader named William J. Murray III protested against the practice on the grounds that it offended his beliefs as an atheist. He and his mother, outspoken, controversy-provoking Madalyn Murray, believed that the Bible was "nauseating, historically inaccurate, replete with the ravings of madness."

Mrs. Murray had been attracted by atheism at the age of thirteen, after reading the Bible and finding it "unbelievable." She decided to bring the suit, she explained, after her son Bill, lately turned fourteen, came to her and said, "Look, either you follow your convictions or you're a hypocrite. Do I have to pray in school or not?"

At Bill's urging, Mrs. Murray wrote to the Baltimore School Board, requesting that her son be allowed to leave the room during the five-minute religious exercise. When this request was rejected by the school superintendent, she took Bill out of school for two weeks. The board later agreed to permit nonbelievers to leave the classroom during religious exercises. By that time Mrs. Murray had resolved to challenge the constitutionality of the exercises themselves.

The lower courts in Maryland ruled against the Murrays, and the Supreme Court agreed to review their case, along with that of the Schempp family.* Some observers expected that after the criticism to which it had been subjected as a result of its first school-prayer decision, the high Court would take the opportunity presented by these new cases to back down somewhat and rule that voluntary religious services in the schools did not violate the Constitution. But, on the contrary, the Court reaffirmed its earlier ruling in strong terms.

* *Abington School District v. Schempp; Murray v. Curlett,* 374 U.S. 203 (1963).

Justice Clark delivered the Court's opinion. After reviewing the history of the Establishment Clause and the importance of the principle of the separation of church and state, he wrote:

> The place of religion in our society is an exalted one, achieved through a long tradition of reliance on the home, the church, and the inviolable citadel of the individual heart and mind. We have come to recognize through bitter experience that it is not within the power of government to invade that citadel, whether its purpose or effect be to aid or oppose, to advance or retard. In the relationship between man and religion, the State is firmly committed to a position of neutrality.

In his dissent, Justice Stewart emphasized that as long as no school child was forced to pray, in his view the First Amendment was not violated:

> What our Constitution indispensably protects is the freedom of each of us, be he Jew or Agnostic, Christian or Atheist, Buddhist or Freethinker, to believe or disbelieve, to worship or not worship, to pray or keep silent, according to his own conscience uncoerced and unconstrained by government.

He suggested that school boards could continue to permit religious exercises, with provisions for children who did not wish to participate.

But he was alone. In support of the ruling of Justice Clark, a Protestant, there were concurring opinions by Justice Brennan, a Catholic, and by Justice Goldberg, a Jew. In his lengthy opinion, Justice William J. Brennan, Jr., attempted to distinguish between impermissible religious exercises sponsored by government bodies and permissible activities, such as the use of the motto In God We Trust, which have lost their original religious meaning and have been adopted as state ceremonies. Justice Brennan also stressed the need for "strict neutrality" in the state's attitude toward religion.

Justice Arthur J. Goldberg, joined by Justice John M. Harlan, discussed the delicacy of the judgment required in dealing with the relations between state and church. He held, for example, that supplying chaplains to men in the armed forces who wanted their services was a permissible activity of the government. As for schools, he observed that there was no restriction on teaching *about* religion; what was unconstitutional was engaging the students in an actual religious exercise.

In a separate concurring opinion, Justice Douglas interpreted the Establishment Clause most stringently to mean that the state might not use any of its funds to promote any religious beliefs.

So the Murrays had won their case. But it was a very costly victory for them. Mrs. Murray lost her job; stores refused to give her credit; her two sons were beaten up repeatedly by gangs of boys while the case was in the courts. "Let me tell you what my Christian neighbors have done," said the articulate Mrs. Murray to a reporter. "Every window has been broken at least once. We've been rotten-egged. Trees have been broken off, azaleas and irises pulled up, roses stepped on. . . . For us to have a little beauty in our home, to somehow live normally is something my neighbors cannot stand. Our

THE RIGHTS OF THE PEOPLE

automobile has been vandalized time and again. Windows have been broken, tires slashed. There's even been a bullet through the side."

Mrs. Murray received thousands of threats and scurrilous letters on the order of the following: "You filthy atheist. Only a rat like you would go to court to stop prayer. All curses on you and your family. Bad luck and leprosy disease upon you and your damn family." Madalyn Murray's ancestors had landed in Massachusetts in 1650; yet, after winning her case in the courts, she found herself subjected to so much harassment that she fled to Hawaii.

Still, she carried on her anti-religion campaign: "I want to be able to walk down any street in America and not see a cross or any other sign of religion. I won't stop till the Pope—or whoever the highest religious authority is—says atheists have a right to breathe in this world." Such sentiments, colorfully expressed, aroused religious people throughout the country against her—until she could claim, with reasonable accuracy, that she was "the most hated woman in America."

This was not the first time in our history that the courts had come to the defense of an unpopular person in behalf of an important principle. The Bill of Rights has often been used to protect a small—and often widely detested—minority from the power of the overwhelming majority. For hard experience has taught that where an unpopular minority's rights are not secure, then the rights of everyone are in jeopardy.

THE WALL BETWEEN CHURCH AND STATE

The issue in the Murray case was not whether the Justices shared Mrs. Murray's anti-religious views or liked the language in which she chose to express them. The issue was whether Bill Murray's rights under the Constitution were being invaded by school authorities. In deciding this case as it did, the Warren Court bolstered the walls of separation between church and state.

McCollum v.
Board of Education
1948

BLACK	OPINION OF COURT
REED	Dissenting opinion
FRANKFURTER	Concurring opinion
DOUGLAS	Concurred
JACKSON	Concurring opinion (also joined Frankfurter)
BURTON	Concurred (joined Black-Frankfurter)
CLARK	
MINTON	
WARREN	
HARLAN	
BRENNAN	
WHITTAKER	
STEWART	
WHITE	
GOLDBERG	
FORTAS	
MARSHALL	

Justices Rutledge,
Vinson, and Murphy
also concurred

Zorach v. Clauson 1952	Engel v. Vitale 1962	Abington v. Schempp 1963
Dissenting opinion	OPINION OF COURT	Concurred
Concurred		
Dissenting opinion	Did not participate	
OPINION OF COURT	Concurring opinion	Concurring opinion
Dissented		
Concurred		
Concurred	Concurred	OPINION OF COURT
Concurred		
	Concurred	Concurred
	Concurred	Concurred (joined Goldberg)
	Concurred	Concurring opinion
	Dissenting opinion	Dissenting opinion
	Did not participate	Concurred
		Concurring opinion

Justice Vinson also concurred

III | THE RIGHTS OF SUSPECTED CRIMINALS

> *In all criminal prosecutions, the accused shall . . . have the Assistance of Counsel for his defence.*

In no country of the world is a person accused of a crime entitled to more rights than in the United States. The suspect or defendant in a criminal case who knows what his rights are and has the means to take advantage of them need not fear that he will be railroaded to prison without having had a chance to confront his accusers and tell his side of the story. But a great many of the persons arrested in this country on serious criminal charges—perhaps most of them—are not fully aware of their rights and do not have the money to hire the best legal help. It was in behalf of these defendants that the Supreme Court broke new ground with a memorable set of decisions that are still being debated throughout the country.

The first—and in several ways the most remarkable—of these cases reached the Court in 1962, in the form of a neatly hand-printed letter from a convict in Florida asking that his conviction be reviewed. The convict, Clarence Earl Gideon, was a fifty-one-year-old petty thief, drifter, and gambler who had spent most of his adult life in various jails for burglary and larceny. In June 1961 he was arrested in Panama City, Florida. He was charged with breaking into a poolroom one night to steal beer, Coke, and coins from a cigarette machine.

From the beginning, Gideon maintained his innocence. Appearing in a Florida courtroom in August 1961, he told the judge that he was not prepared to go on trial because he had no lawyer, and he requested that the court appoint counsel to represent him. Most states, along with the federal government, did guarantee lawyers for indigent defendants—but at the time Florida, like several other states in the South, did not. The Panama City judge replied: "Mr. Gideon, I am sorry, but I cannot appoint counsel to represent you in this case. Under the laws of the State of Florida, the only time the court can appoint counsel to represent a defendant is when that person is charged with a capital offense. I am sorry, but I will have to deny your request to appoint counsel to defend you in this case."

Gideon went on to attempt to conduct his own defense. He did his best—but his best was not good enough. He was found guilty and given the maximum five-year sentence. After his conviction he appealed to

THE RIGHTS OF SUSPECTED CRIMINALS

the Florida Supreme Court, which denied him a hearing. Then he turned to the U.S. Supreme Court.

The high Court permits persons who have no money of their own to file requests for a hearing without going through the normal costly preliminaries. Each year hundreds of such pleas arrive from prisons throughout the land, but only a handful are found worthy of the Court's attention. Gideon's appeal was one of these few, for his case afforded the Justices an opportunity to reconsider the question of whether the phrase in the Sixth Amendment that guarantees a person accused of a crime "the assistance of counsel for his defense" should be applied to state courts as well as to federal courts.

In his original request for a lawyer, Gideon told the Florida judge: "The United States Supreme Court says I am entitled to be represented by counsel."

In fact, the Supreme Court had made quite a different ruling. In 1942 it had been faced with a case very similar to Gideon's. An unemployed farm hand in Maryland named Smith Betts, charged with robbery, asked the judge to appoint a lawyer to defend him. The judge explained that it was the custom in that county to appoint lawyers for indigent defendants only in capital cases. Forced to conduct his own defense, Betts failed and was sentenced to eight years' imprisonment. Like thousands of other penniless defendants, he was fated to serve a long prison term without ever having had the aid of a lawyer.

When his appeal reached the Supreme Court, a 6 to 3

majority decided against him.* Justice Owen J. Roberts, delivering the Court's opinion, pointed out "that, in the great majority of states, it has been the considered judgment of the people, their representatives, and their courts that appointment of counsel is not a fundamental right, essential to a fair trial." The Court left it up to the legislature of each state to decide whether to provide free legal assistance in any given type of case.

The decision was sharply criticized by legal scholars as well as civil libertarians. In the three-man minority were Justices Black and Douglas, who would still be on the Court more than twenty years later, when Gideon's appeal came before it. In the intervening years, their colleagues gave signs that they were having second thoughts about the validity of the *Betts* decision, and by the 1960's the Warren Court was obviously ready to reverse it and to lay down a quite different rule regarding the right to counsel. It only required Clarence Earl Gideon to give them their opportunity. The drifter and petty criminal who had been successful at so little in life would win this battle, at least.

Having agreed to hear Gideon's appeal (in itself a significant victory for the prisoner), the Justices now had to select an attorney to plead his case before them. It is a long-standing custom of the high Court to appoint lawyers to present the arguments in behalf of indigent persons. Arguing constitutional issues before the nation's final court of appeal—whose nine Justices have a way of interrupting an attorney's presentation to ask

* *Betts v. Brady,* 316 U.S. 455 (1942).

THE RIGHTS OF SUSPECTED CRIMINALS

probing questions—requires considerable skill and experience. It is an honor for an attorney to be selected to plead an important case before the Supreme Court. In choosing Abe Fortas to represent Clarence Gideon, the Justices could hardly have settled on a more prominent or esteemed member of the Washington bar. A former government official and adviser to Presidents, Fortas would a few years later be named to a place on the high bench before which he spoke in behalf of Gideon.

Gideon's case was argued before the Supreme Court in January 1963, and in March came the Court's unanimous decision reversing his conviction.* It was delivered by Justice Black, who thus had the unusual satisfaction of overturning a decision from which he had dissented twenty years before. He wrote:

> ... In our adversary system of criminal justice, any person hailed into court, who is too poor to hire a lawyer, cannot be assured a fair trial unless counsel is provided for him. This seems to us to be an obvious truth. Governments, both state and federal, quite properly spend vast sums of money to establish machinery to try defendants accused of crime. Lawyers to prosecute are everywhere deemed essential to protect the public's interest in an orderly society. Similarly, there are few defendants charged with crime, few indeed, who fail to hire the best lawyers they can get to prepare and present their defense. That government hires lawyers to prosecute and defendants who have the money hire lawyers to defend are the strongest indications of the widespread belief that lawyers in criminal courts are necessities, not luxuries. The right of one charged with crime to counsel may

* *Gideon v. Wainwright,* 372 U.S. 335 (1963).

not be deemed fundamental and essential to fair trials in some countries, but it is in ours. From the beginning, our state and national constitutions and laws have laid great emphasis on procedural and substantive safeguards designed to assure fair trials before impartial tribunals in which every defendant stands equal before the law. This noble ideal cannot be realized if the poor man charged with crime has to face his accusers without a lawyer to assist him.

Hereafter, as a result of this decision, the Sixth Amendment guarantee of assistance of counsel to an accused would apply to state courts as well as federal courts.

For Clarence Gideon, the decision meant a new trial —in which he had a competent lawyer. As he said afterwards, "Everything at the new trial looked the same, the same courtroom, the same judge. But there was a difference; I had an attorney." His attorney did such a good job of cross-examining the main witness against his client that Gideon won acquittal. In addition, hundreds of other prisoners who had been convicted without benefit of defense counsel won their release from Florida jails, and the Florida state legislature belatedly enacted a public-defender law, so that attorneys would be made available to penniless defendants.

As Anthony Lewis of *The New York Times* wrote in his book on the case, Gideon's triumph "shows that the poorest and least powerful of men—a convict with not even a friend to visit him in prison—can take his cause to the highest court in the land and bring about a fundamental change in the law."

THE RIGHTS OF SUSPECTED CRIMINALS

Like other major legal decisions, the *Gideon* decision resolved one issue but opened up others. It was now settled that every defendant was entitled to be represented by a lawyer at his trial. But what of the period before his trial, when he is in police custody and undergoing questioning? Does he have a right to a lawyer at that time as well?

The Court confronted this question in 1964, when it agreed to review the case of Danny Escobedo. In 1960, Escobedo, a short, skinny twenty-two-year-old with a history of delinquency ("I never was the ideal teenager," he conceded), was picked up by Chicago police on suspicion that he had been involved in the murder of his sister's husband.

There had been no witnesses to the murder—a shot in the back on a cold January night—and no weapon was found. Searching for leads, the police took into custody Escobedo, his sister, and two friends. They were questioned for more than fourteen hours at police headquarters before a lawyer called in by the mother of one of the friends obtained their release.

The police still had their suspicions, however, and after further interrogation, one of the friends accused Danny Escobedo of having committed the crime. He was arrested, handcuffed, and taken into the police-interrogation room for questioning. As he later recalled, the "detectives said they had us pretty well, up pretty tight, and we might as well admit to this crime." He was not told that he had the right to remain silent or to call for an attorney. Nevertheless, he said, "I am sorry, but I would like to have advice from my lawyer." When the lawyer arrived at the station house, the police refused to let him see Escobedo, despite repeated requests, from 9:30 P.M. on the night of the arrest until 1 A.M. the following morning. Escobedo, meanwhile, was told by the police that the lawyer didn't want to see him.

Finally, confronted with the friend who had charged him with the murder, Escobedo shouted, "You did it!" thereby admitting that he himself had some knowledge of the crime. After several hours of further questioning, he confessed that he had offered the friend five hundred dollars to kill his brother-in-law. He later retracted this statement, explaining that he had been given to understand by the police that he would be permitted to go home if he pinned the actual killing on his friend; but the judge at his trial ruled that the confession had been voluntary, and Danny Escobedo was convicted and sentenced to twenty years' imprisonment. (The friend received a life sentence.)

After two years in prison, Escobedo filed a pauper's appeal to the Illinois Supreme Court. A competent young lawyer was appointed to argue his case and, in 1962, the Illinois court reversed his conviction on the grounds that, during the police investigation, he had been promised by a detective that he would be allowed to go free if he confessed. On a rehearing, however, the state court reversed itself, and Escobedo's lawyer took his appeal to the U.S. Supreme Court.

A person arrested by the FBI, the federal government's police arm, is told, as a matter of routine, that he has a right to remain silent and to see a lawyer. It was now up to the high Court to decide whether this long-standing rule should be applied to state and local police as well. In June 1964 the Court reached its decision—and after having served four and a half years in prison, Danny Escobedo went free.*

In his ruling, Justice Goldberg emphasized that when Escobedo was questioned the second time and was denied a chance to consult with a lawyer, the police were no longer conducting a general investigation of an unsolved crime; they were focusing on one suspect, Danny Escobedo, with the purpose of getting him to make a confession. He was probably not aware that under Illinois law an admission of complicity in a murder plot was equivalent to an admission that he had himself fired the shot, and he had no attorney to explain this vital point to him. For all practical purposes, in Justice Goldberg's view, at his second interrogation Escobedo had already been charged with murder, and if his rights were not safeguarded at that critical point, then he could not hope for a fair trial later. Justice Goldberg wrote:

We hold, therefore, that where, as here, the investigation is no longer a general inquiry into an unsolved crime but has begun to focus on a particular suspect, the suspect has been taken into police custody, the police carry out a process of interrogations that lends itself to eliciting incriminating statements, the suspect has requested and been denied an opportunity to consult with his lawyer, and the police have not

* *Escobedo v. Illinois,* 378 U.S. 478 (1964).

effectively warned him of his absolute constitutional right to remain silent, the accused has been denied "the Assistance of Counsel" in violation of the Sixth Amendment to the Constitution . . . and that no statement elicited by the police during the interrogation may be used against him at any criminal trial. . . .

Taking note of the concern that the number of confessions would decrease dramatically as a result of this ruling, and law-enforcement efforts would therefore be hampered, Justice Goldberg replied that it is precisely because confessions are so common in the period between arrest and indictment that precautions must be taken to make certain that they are indeed voluntary. Our Constitution, he noted, "strikes the balance in favor of the right of the accused to be advised by his lawyer of his privilege against self-incrimination." Justice Goldberg went on:

We have learned the lesson of history, ancient and modern, that a system of criminal law enforcement which comes to depend on the "confession" will, in the long run, be less reliable and more subject to abuses than a system which depends on extrinsic evidence, independently secured through skillful investigation.

The decision in the *Escobedo* case was not unanimous, as it had been in *Gideon*. Four Justices—White, Clark, Stewart, and Harlan—dissented.

Justice Byron R. White acknowledged the importance of making certain that an accused person is informed of his right to remain silent and of the fact that anything he says may be used against him. He held, however, that a lawyer's presence was not essential to guarantee these rights and that the rule laid down by the majority would prove "wholly unworkable and impossible to administer unless police cars are equipped with public defenders, and undercover agents and police informants have defense counsel at their side."

He carried the ruling of the majority out to what he felt was its absurd conclusion: "Under this new approach, one might just as well argue that a potential defendant is constitutionally entitled to a lawyer before, not after, he commits a crime, since it is then that crucial incriminating evidence is put within the reach of the government by the would-be accused." Justice White feared that law enforcement would be "crippled" by the new rule, and "its task made a great deal more difficult...."

Justice Harlan agreed: "I think the rule is most ill-conceived and that it seriously and unjustifiedly fetters perfectly legitimate methods of criminal enforcement."

And Justice Stewart, too, expressed concern over the "untold and highly unfortunate impact today's decision may have upon the fair administration of criminal justice."

Despite the vigorous dissents, however, the majority of the Court was prepared to go even further than it had already to guarantee an individual the right to a lawyer virtually from the moment he is brought to the police station. This it found an opportunity to do in 1966, when faced with four cases in which men had confessed to crimes without first being told that they had a right to consult with an attorney. The cases, which involved robbery, kidnaping, and murder, originated in New York, Kansas, California, and Arizona. All the defendants were convicted. All appealed.

The defendant whose name is best remembered from this set of cases is Ernesto Arthur Miranda. Miranda, twenty-three years old when he was arrested in Phoenix, Arizona, in 1963, on charges of kidnaping and raping an eighteen-year-old girl, had never completed high school and did not hold a regular job. At the police station, the girl identified Miranda as her assailant, and after two hours of questioning by police, he wrote out his confession. The confession was admitted as evidence at his trial, despite the objections of his attorney that Miranda had never been told that he had a right to consult a lawyer prior to answering any questions; nor had he been told that he had a right to remain silent. He was found guilty and sentenced to twenty to thirty years in prison.

An appeal was brought before the Arizona Supreme Court, which turned it down. The judges of the Arizona court noted that Miranda (unlike Danny Escobedo) had never specifically asked for a lawyer after his arrest. And so the *Miranda* case, along with three others that raised similar issues, reached the U.S. Supreme Court.*

In setting forth the opinion of the majority, Chief Justice Warren noted that "an understanding of the

* *Miranda v. Arizona,* 384 U.S. 436 (1966).

nature and setting of in-custody interrogation is essential to our decisions today." And then he went on to analyze a typical scene of a suspect being questioned by the police:

> To be alone with the subject is essential to prevent distraction and to deprive him of any outside support. The aura of confidence in his guilt undermines his will to resist. He merely confirms the preconceived story the police seem to have him describe. Patience and persistence, at times relentless questioning, are employed. . . . When normal procedures fail to produce the needed result, the police may resort to deceptive stratagems such as giving false legal advice. It is important to keep the subject off balance, for example, by trading on his insecurity about himself or his surroundings. The police then persuade, trick, or cajole him out of exercising his constitutional rights.
>
> It is obvious that such an interrogation environment is created for no purpose other than to subjugate the individual to the will of his examiner. The atmosphere carries its own badge of intimidation. To be sure, this is not physical intimidation, but it is equally destructive of human dignity. The current practice of incommunicado interrogation [when the prisoner is not permitted to communicate with anyone but the police] is at odds with one of our Nation's most cherished principles—that the individual may not be compelled to incriminate himself. Unless adequate protective devices are employed to dispel the compulsion inherent in custodial surroundings, no statement obtained from the defendant can truly be the product of free choice.

Focusing on the fundamental right of every person against self-incrimination, Justice Warren presented the accused party's plight in very human terms:

An individual swept from familiar surroundings into police custody, surrounded by antagonistic forces, and subjected to the technique of persuasion described above cannot be otherwise than under compulsion to speak. As a practical matter, the compulsion to speak in the isolated setting of the police station may well be greater than in courts or other official investigations, where there are often impartial observers to guard against intimidation or trickery. . . .

Having made the point that ordinary police procedures may readily violate a defendant's constitutional rights under the Fifth Amendment, Justice Warren set down a number of safeguards that must henceforward be observed in police interrogations:

At the outset, if a person in custody is to be subjected to interrogation, he must first be informed in clear and unequivocal terms that he has the right to remain silent. . . . The warning of the right to remain silent must be accompanied by the explanation that anything said can and will be used against the individual in court . . . the right to have counsel present at the interrogation is indispensable to the protection of the Fifth Amendment privilege.

Accordingly, the Court ruled that a suspect being held for questioning must be clearly informed that he has a right to have a lawyer by his side while being questioned. If he lacks the money to hire a lawyer, then —ruled the Court—he must be informed that a lawyer will be appointed to represent him if he so desires.

To leave no doubt as to the Court's determination that the rights of suspects may not be slighted, Justice Warren wrote: "If the individual indicates in any manner, at any time prior to or during questioning, that he wishes to remain silent, the interrogation must cease. . . . If the individual states that he wants an attorney, the interrogation must cease until an attorney is present."

Again, as in the Escobedo case, four Justices—Clark, Harlan, Stewart, and White—registered strong dissents.

Arguing angrily that the Court's decision "represents poor constitutional law and entails harmful consequences for the country at large," Justice Harlan observed:

Legal history has been stretched before to satisfy deep needs of society. In this instance, however, the Court has not and cannot make the powerful showing that its new rules are plainly desirable in the context of our society, something which is surely demanded before those rules are engrafted onto the Constitution and imposed on every State and county in the land.

Pointing out that Miranda's confession had been obtained during a relatively brief daytime questioning by two officers, without any unfairness or the use of force, and that it was done for a legitimate purpose, Justice Harlan wrote:

What the Court largely ignores is that its rules impair, if they will not eventually serve wholly to frustrate, an instrument of law enforcement that has long and quite reasonably been thought worth the price paid for it. There can be little doubt that the Court's new code would markedly decrease the number of confessions. . . . The social costs of crime are too great to call the rules anything but a hazardous experimentation.

THE RIGHTS OF THE PEOPLE

The dissenters felt that the safety of the society should be placed above the absolute right of every suspect to a lawyer. Justice White warned: "In some unknown number of cases, the Court's rule will return a killer, a rapist, or other criminal to the streets . . . to repeat his crime whenever it pleases him." He concluded: "I have no desire whatsoever to share the responsibility for any such impact on the present criminal process."*

Ernesto Miranda's victory in the Supreme Court did not do him much immediate good, since he had been convicted of another robbery and so remained in jail. Danny Escobedo was released but continued to run into difficulties with the Chicago police.

As to whether all confessions obtained by police around the country before the *Escobedo* and *Miranda* decisions might now be appealed, the Supreme Court ruled that they could not, because that "would seriously disrupt the administration of our criminal laws. It would require the retrial or release of numerous prisoners found guilty by trustworthy evidence in conformity with previously announced constitutional standards."

---

* In February 1970, the Supreme Court, whose membership had changed significantly since 1966, modified the impact of *Miranda*. In a five-to-four decision, the Court ruled that a statement made by a suspect who had not been warned of his rights by the police might nevertheless be used by the prosecution in his trial to contradict his testimony. The opinion was delivered by Chief Justice Warren E. Burger, who was joined by Justice Harry A. Blackmun and Justices Harlan, Stewart, and White. Justices Brennan, Black, Douglas, and Marshall dissented. Justice Brennan wrote that the new decision "goes far toward undoing much of the progress made in conforming police methods to the Constitution."

THE RIGHTS OF SUSPECTED CRIMINALS

The Court's critics, however, were not mollified by the news that the decisions would not be retroactive, and the words of the dissenting Justices came to seem mild in the uproar that followed the *Miranda* case.

Political conservatives, long opposed to the spirit of the Warren Court, were in the forefront of the new assault.

A Senator from Nevada declared: "It seems to me that we have become obsessed with uncovering new rights and safeguards for the criminal to such a degree that we have unbalanced the scales of justice, and find ourselves in the unenviable position of losing control of the crime and violence that are running rampant in our cities."

A Senator from North Carolina agreed that the scales of justice were being tilted "in favor of self-confessed criminals and against society and the victims of crimes."

The Mayor of Los Angeles commented after the *Miranda* ruling: "This decision deprives us of the cooperation of the person who knows most about the crime—the one who committed it—and puts the handcuffs on the police instead of on the criminal."

And a police chief in Texas was exasperated: "It's the damndest thing I ever heard—we may as well close up shop."

The press, too, had its share of vehement critics. An article in the *Reader's Digest* entitled "Let's Have Justice for Non-Criminals Too" charged in 1966 that the Court "has progressively handcuffed the police, turned trial judges into automatons, and blindfolded juries, all to the immense benefit of criminals."

As might be expected, civil-liberties lawyers saw the Court's rulings in quite a different light. Escobedo's attorney observed: "This decision means that the poor, uneducated, and uninformed can now enjoy the rights that were previously only enjoyed by the wealthy and sophisticated."

As it turned out, the warnings to suspects of their rights, as ordered by the Court, does not seem to have noticeably affected the number of confessions. In Detroit, for example, it was found, after a year of notifying suspects of their rights to silence and to a lawyer, that confessions were obtained in 56 per cent of murder cases, compared to 53 per cent during a period when no warnings were offered.

The District Attorney of Los Angeles County noted in a study on the impact of the *Miranda* decision: "The most significant things about our findings are that suspects will talk regardless of the warnings, and furthermore, it isn't so all-fired important whether they talk or not."

So the fears about the impact of the Court's ruling seem to have been exaggerated. The whole question of this impact on the incidence of crime was put into a different perspective in 1966 by Ramsey Clark, then Deputy Attorney General of the United States, as well as son of one of the dissenting Justices. Clark commented:

Court rules do not cause crime. People do not commit crimes because they know they cannot be questioned by the police before presentiment, or even because they feel they will not be convicted. We as a people commit crimes because we are capable of committing crimes. We choose to commit crimes.

Not a very satisfactory analysis, perhaps, but it does suggest that in seeking to understand the causes of crime, it is simple-minded to lay the blame on a scapegoat such as the Supreme Court.

	Betts v. Brady 1942
BLACK	Dissenting opinion
REED	Concurred
FRANKFURTER	Concurred
DOUGLAS	Dissented (joined Black)
JACKSON	Concurred
BURTON	
CLARK	
MINTON	
WARREN	
HARLAN	
BRENNAN	
WHITTAKER	
STEWART	
WHITE	
GOLDBERG	
FORTAS	
MARSHALL	

Justice Roberts wrote the opinion of the Court. Justices Stone and Byrnes concurred, and Justice Murphy dissented

Gideon v. Wainwright 1963	Escobedo v. Illinois 1964	Miranda v. Arizona 1966
OPINION OF COURT	Concurred	Concurred
Concurring opinion	Concurred	Concurred
Concurring opinion	Dissented (joined White)	Dissenting opinion
Concurred	Concurred	OPINION OF COURT
Concurring opinion	Dissenting opinion	Dissenting opinion (and joined White)
Concurred	Concurred	Concurred
Concurred	Dissenting opinion (and joined White)	Dissented (joined White)
Concurred	Dissenting opinion	Dissenting opinion
Concurred	OPINION OF COURT	
		Concurred

IV | THE YOUNG HAVE RIGHTS, TOO

> ... *Nor shall any State deprive any person of life, liberty, or property, without due process of law.* ...

In addition to delivering a notable series of decisions designed to safeguard the rights of suspects from abuse by the police, the Warren Court made an important ruling regarding the rights of juvenile offenders.

Our state courts have long recognized that children who become involved with the law require special treatment, to save them from overly harsh punishment and a possible future in crime. Since Illinois adopted a juvenile court statute in 1899, every state in the Union has followed suit. In every state, regulations have been devised which give juvenile-court authorities wide discretion in dealing with youngsters—in theory, for the youngsters' benefit. However, it has not always turned out that way.

As Justice Abe Fortas described the development:

The early reformers were appalled by adult procedures and penalties, and by the fact that children could be given long sentences and mixed in jail with hardened criminals. . . . They believed that society's role was not to ascertain whether the child was "guilty" or "innocent" but "What is he, how has he become what he is, and what had best be done in his interest and in the interest of the state to save him from a downward career." The child—essentially good, as they saw it—was to be made "to feel that he is the object of [the State's] care and solicitude," not that he was under arrest or on trial. . . . The idea of crime and punishment was to be abandoned. The child was to be "treated" and "rehabilitated" and the procedures, from apprehension through institutionalization, were to be "clinical rather than punitive."

The state, in short, was to act not as the defendant's adversary, as it ordinarily does in criminal cases, but as *parens patriae,* substitute government parents. As an expert on juvenile law at Columbia University Law School put it, "The reformers who drafted the original juvenile court act in 1899 had the notion that they could create an institution . . . in which children would have everyone on their side and therefore no need for lawyers. . . . That notion turned out to be false. . . ."

There is no doubt that the special provisions applied to youngsters were adopted with the best of intentions—but, as the high Court discovered, our juvenile courts were not working well in practice. Many were run by judges who had little education or little skill in dealing with children; juvenile crime was on the increase; many convicted juveniles went on to commit new crimes; courts tended to be overcrowded and unsympathetic.

THE YOUNG HAVE RIGHTS, TOO

And, most significantly, the latitude allowed local judges in the nation's three thousand juvenile courts was in fact depriving many youthful defendants of their constitutional rights.

The legal difficulties of fifteen-year-old Gerald Francis Gault began at 10 A.M., Monday, June 8, 1964, when he and a friend were taken into custody by the sheriff of Gila County, Arizona, after a neighbor had complained that the boys had called her on the telephone and made lewd and indecent remarks. Both Gerald's parents were at work in their desert mining town of Globe when he was picked up, and they were not notified as to his whereabouts. They finally tracked him down that evening at the County Detention Home.

At a highly informal hearing before a judge the following day, the woman who had made the complaint was not present. No witnesses were sworn, and no transcript was made of the proceedings. Later the police officer in the case and the presiding judge would say that Gerald had admitted that he made the remarks on the phone. His mother, on the other hand, maintained that he only admitted dialing the woman's number, not speaking. So vague were the records in the case that there is even disagreement as to the day that Gerald was released from the Detention Home.

At another hearing on June 15, Gerald—a high-school dropout who was still on six months' probation for being in the company of a boy who had been found guilty in February of taking a wallet from a woman's purse—said he had only dialed the number. Despite his mother's request that the complaining woman be called "so she could see which boy had done the talking, the dirty talking over the phone," the woman never appeared.

If Gerald had been an adult and had been found guilty of the offense in question, under the Arizona Criminal Code he could have been fined from five to fifty dollars and sentenced to imprisonment for not more than two months. But Gerald was not an adult and so the Criminal Code did not apply in his case. The judge used his discretion to sentence the boy, whom he described as "a delinquent child," to confinement in the State Industrial School until he reached the age of twenty-one—that is, for *six years.*

As Arizona law permits no appeal from a judge's ruling in juvenile cases, Gerald's parents, assisted by Civil Liberties Union attorneys, asked the Arizona courts for a writ of *habeas corpus*—which would have gotten Gerald a court hearing to determine if he had been justly imprisoned. The courts denied the request and the Gaults appealed to the Supreme Court. This, then, became the case of *In re Gault,* which means literally, "in the matter of Gault," a phrase used when there are no directly contending parties to a suit. In Gerald Gault's case, application for a court hearing was being made on his behalf because he was a minor.

The significance of the case went far beyond Gerald Gault, who was, in fact, freed on probation after six months in the State Industrial School. In 1965, the year

THE YOUNG HAVE RIGHTS, TOO

after Gerald's arrest, 601,000 children under the age of eighteen came before America's juvenile courts. One out of five of the persons arrested for serious crimes that year was a juvenile. Whatever the high Court decided in Gerald's case would have application to the other hundreds of thousands of youths who found themselves in trouble with the law each year.

Gerald's lawyers argued that he had been denied six basic rights given to all persons charged with crimes by the Due Process Clause of the Fourteenth Amendment:

1. He was not given timely notice of the charges against him.

2. He was not offered the opportunity to engage an attorney.

3. He was not permitted to confront his accuser or to have her subjected to cross-examination.

4. He was not given the privilege, guaranteed by the Fifth Amendment, of not testifying against himself.

5. He was not allowed to see a transcript of the proceedings which resulted in his imprisonment.

6. He was denied the right of a review of his case by a higher court.

The Supreme Court agreed that Gerald Gault's rights had been blatantly violated.* The theme of Justice Fortas's closely reasoned decision was that "neither the Fourteenth Amendment nor the Bill of Rights is for adults alone." Emphasizing that "due process of law is

* *In re Gault,* 387 U.S. 1 (1967).

the primary and indispensable foundation of individual freedom," he observed that by avoiding established principles of due process (even for the most benevolent motives), our juvenile courts have not always treated children fairly, efficiently, or effectively. He described the experience of Gerald Gault:

A boy is charged with misconduct. The boy is committed to an institution where he may be restrained for years. It is of no constitutional consequence—and of limited practical meaning—that the institution to which he is committed is called an Industrial School. The fact of the matter is that, however euphemistic the title, a "receiving home" or an "industrial school" for juveniles is an institution of confinement in which the child is incarcerated for a greater or lesser time. His world becomes "a building with whitewashed walls, regimented routine, and institutional laws . . ." instead of mother and father and sisters and brothers and friends and classmates, his world is peopled by guards, custodians, state employees, and "delinquents" confined with him for anything from waywardness to rape and homicide. . . . The essential difference between Gerald's case and a normal criminal case is that safeguards available to adults were discarded in Gerald's case. The summary procedure as well as the long commitment were possible because Gerald was fifteen years of age instead of over eighteen.

Justice Fortas addressed himself to the points raised by Gerald's attorneys:

Notice of Charges: "Due process does not allow a hearing to be held in which a youth's freedom and his parents' right to his custody are at stake without giving them timely notice, in advance of the hearing, of the specific issues that they must meet."

Right to Counsel: "The juvenile needs the assistance of counsel to cope with problems of law, to make skilled inquiry into the facts, to insist upon regularity of the proceedings, and to ascertain whether he has a defense and to prepare and submit it."

Self-incrimination: "It would indeed be surprising if the privilege against self-incrimination were available to hardened criminals but not to children. . . . If counsel is not present for some permissible reason when an admission is obtained, the greatest care must be taken to assure that the admission was voluntary, in the sense not only that it has not been coerced or suggested, but also that it is not the product of ignorance of rights or of adolescent fantasy, fright, or despair. . . ."

Justices Black and White wrote concurring opinions, and Justice Harlan concurred in part and dissented in part. The only entirely dissenting opinion came from Justice Stewart, who called the Court's decision "wholly unsound as a matter of constitutional law, and sadly unwise as a matter of judicial policy." Justice Stewart took pains to spell out the differences between an ordinary criminal court and the nation's juvenile courts:

Juvenile proceedings are not criminal trials. They are not civil trials. They are simply not adversary proceedings. Whether treating with a delinquent child, a neglected child, a defective child, or a dependent child, a juvenile proceeding's whole purpose and mission is the very opposite of the mission and purpose of a prosecution in a criminal court. The object of the one is correction of a condition. The object of the other is conviction and punishment for a criminal act.

But the other Justices were not persuaded. In his concurring opinion, Justice Black spelled out the actual results of the juvenile-court procedures in Gerald Gault's case:

> As a juvenile . . . he was put through a more or less secret, informal hearing by the court, after which he was ordered, or more realistically, "sentenced" to confinement in Arizona's Industrial School until he reaches twenty-one years of age. Thus, in a juvenile system designed to lighten or avoid punishment for criminality, he was ordered by the State to six years' confinement in what is in all but name a penitentiary or jail.

From the facts of this case, Justice Black arrived at an important generalization:

> Where a person, infant or adult, can be seized by the State, charged and convicted for violating a State law, and then ordered by the State to be confined for six years, I think the Constitution requires that he be tried in accordance with the guarantees of all the provisions of the Bill of Rights.

And such was the import of the Supreme Court's decision in the matter of young Gerald Gault.

In re Gault
1967

BLACK	Concurring opinion
REED	
FRANKFURTER	
DOUGLAS	Concurred
JACKSON	
BURTON	
CLARK	Concurred
MINTON	
WARREN	Concurred
HARLAN	Opinion concurring in part, dissenting in part
BRENNAN	Concurred
WHITTAKER	
STEWART	Dissenting opinion
WHITE	Concurred
GOLDBERG	
FORTAS	OPINION OF COURT
MARSHALL	

V | THE ZONE OF PRIVACY

> *The right of the people to be secure in their persons, houses, papers, and effects, against unreasonable searches and seizures, shall not be violated....*

In November 1961 an unusual arrest took place in New Haven, Connecticut. Ordinarily, criminals commit crimes in the dark of night, but the "crime" in Connecticut was committed openly; the "criminals" were proud of what they were doing. Ordinarily, criminals are not the most admired members of their community; they tend to have police records and bad reputations. The offenders in this case were eminently respectable, welcome additions to any community. Ordinarily, criminals do their utmost to stay out of the path of the police after the crime and, if they do meet, relations do not tend to be cordial. In this case, arrest was expected—and desired. The district attorney gave the offenders the choice of turning themselves in quietly or being picked up by a paddy wagon, with photographers along; they chose the quiet way.

The two persons arrested in Connecticut were Mrs. Estelle Griswold, a woman in her sixties who had made a career in social work and was at the time executive director of the Planned Parenthood League of Connecticut, and Dr. C. Lee Buxton, chairman of the department of obstetrics and gynecology at Yale University, former Navy commander, and father of four. Their "crime" consisted of operating a family-planning clinic, mainly for poor families, in violation of a Connecticut law against birth control. They were forcing the authorities to arrest them in order to test the constitutionality of the law.

The importance of such test cases in our judicial system can hardly be overstated. If a law is passed that seems to violate the rights of an individual or a group under the Constitution, how is a citizen to challenge it? One way, of course, is to mount a campaign in the Congress or in a state legislature for the law's repeal, and such campaigns had in fact been attempted annually against the Connecticut anti-birth-control statute—without success. Even if a law is repealed, however, the question of whether it was constitutional in the first place remains undecided, and there is always the possibility that if the political winds should shift, a similar law might be enacted once again. Moreover, a law that is rejected by the legislature of one state may be passed in any or all of the other forty-nine states—unless it is ruled unconstitutional.

THE ZONE OF PRIVACY

It is possible to challenge an existing law by bringing a suit for its repeal—but our courts are reluctant to hear such cases unless there is evidence that the person bringing the suit has been injured by the law. In the birth-control case, Dr. Buxton actually did bring such a suit and the Supreme Court declined to issue a ruling because it seemed that the law was not really being enforced and was in fact a "dead letter." Dr. Buxton himself had suffered no injury. In order to show that the law was indeed still being enforced and that individuals could be very directly affected by it, Dr. Buxton and Mrs. Griswold chose to violate it openly, inviting arrest. In doing so— in risking conviction, a fine, a jail sentence, a blemish on their impeccable records—they were demonstrating their faith in the country's legal system and in the justice of their cause.

The law that Dr. Buxton and Mrs. Griswold set out to test that afternoon in 1961 was an old one, and a strict one. Passed originally in 1879, when attitudes toward sexual behavior were far more restrictive than they are today, the Connecticut statute was the work of New England Puritans, led by the celebrated anti-vice crusader Anthony Comstock. The law, the most stringent of some two dozen birth-control laws around the nation, prohibited not only the sale of contraceptive devices but their use, even by married couples. It was no secret that this prohibition was widely ignored in thousands of otherwise law-abiding homes. A Connecticut doctor described it as being "unenforceable short of having a policeman under every bed in the state."

Whatever was going on in people's bedrooms, however, the police saw to it that no birth-control information or material was openly distributed. Persons of education and means were not affected; they managed to get all the information and material they wanted from their doctors and druggists. Where the law had its greatest impact was on the least-educated, least-affluent parts of the population. That fact troubled Dr. Buxton because, as he pointed out, "were this knowledge as universally shared as the other aspects of our lives, the fears and tensions connected with childbirth might be largely dispelled."

Though this widely ignored, widely criticized law was originated by Puritanical Protestants, it owed its continued existence to the Roman Catholic Church, a powerful political force in Connecticut, where nearly half the residents are Catholic. Polls taken during the 1950's and 1960's showed that young Catholic couples were using birth-control devices to about the same extent as couples of other faiths, but the Church hierarchy held to its position that having children was the prime object of sexual relations and therefore any "artificial" devices designed to prevent conception and procreation were violations of the "natural law."

Most Protestant and Jewish religious leaders did not agree with this stand. They held that in addition to the obvious function of conceiving children, sexual relations between husband and wife were a way of express-

THE ZONE OF PRIVACY

ing love for one another, and hence were good for that reason even if no children resulted. The number of children that married couples wished to have, they maintained, was the business of the husband and wife, not of any church or any state. As a bishop of the Protestant Episcopal Church in California said at the time: "Responsible choice as to the number and spacing of children is simply one of the many areas of life in which people are called upon to make conscientious decisions under God."

Many Catholics, while accepting their Church's view of the subject, nonetheless believed that the Connecticut anti-birth-control law ought to be repealed. They felt that in a land of diverse religions it was improper for any one religious body to impose its moral beliefs on citizens of other faiths. The president of the National Council of Catholic Men called the law "an unwarranted invasion of privacy." Along with Protestant spokesmen, such Catholics argued that the government—in this instance, the State of Connecticut—should not be used as an arm of any church. (A liberal Catholic journalist pointed out that a Catholic legislator in Connecticut could not afford to say a word against the law no matter what he thought of it because he would be charged with being "anti-morality, anti-natural-law, a traitor to the Church, and probably an enemy of God.")

No one objected to the right of Catholic families to follow the moral teachings of their Church; but it was widely argued that non-Catholics should be equally free to follow their beliefs. Private doctors in Connecticut were compelled to recommend and supply birth-control materials surreptitiously, and persons who could not afford a doctor's fee were forced to go to clinics outside their state in order to obtain birth-control information. Dr. Buxton held especially strong feelings on the matter, because several women who had been unable to get birth-control advice had died at his hospital of complications resulting from their pregnancies.

With such considerations in mind, and with the support of medical experts throughout the country, Dr. Buxton and Mrs. Griswold opened a Planned Parenthood clinic in an old mansion in New Haven on November 1, 1961. Nine days later they were arrested, charged with giving married persons information and medical advice on how to prevent conception and with prescribing contraceptive materials for the wife. The fact that they were serving only married couples was, as we shall see, vital for their case. They admitted doing all that they were charged with doing and were convicted and fined one hundred dollars each. (Dr. Buxton observed wryly that considering all the trouble the case had caused him, the judge could at least have fined him more than one hundred dollars.) After their convictions were upheld by two higher courts in Connecticut, the case was accepted for review by the Supreme Court.*

None of the Justices liked the anti-birth-control statute—"an uncommonly silly law," Justice Stewart called it—but the issue before them was not whether they approved or disapproved of it but whether it was in

* *Griswold v. Connecticut,* 381 U.S. 479 (1965).

THE ZONE OF PRIVACY

violation of the U.S. Constitution. To this question, Justice Stewart, along with Justice Black, replied that it was not. "It is the essence of judicial duty," wrote Justice Stewart, "to subordinate our personal views, our own ideas of what legislation is wise and what is not."

Justice Black, who noted that he found the statute "offensive," nonetheless emphasized that the Court does not have the power to invalidate state laws even though they are considered to be "arbitrary, capricious, unreasonable, or oppressive." The Connecticut law on birth control might be all these things and yet not be forbidden by any provision of the federal Constitution. The way to kill such a law, observed Justice Stewart, was for the voters of Connecticut to bring pressure on their state legislators.

But a majority of seven Justices felt otherwise. Delivering the opinion of the Court, Justice Douglas ruled that the Connecticut anti-birth-control statute was unconstitutional because it violated the right to privacy of that state's residents. This was a novel argument, for the Bill of Rights does not include any right to privacy; the word "privacy" is nowhere mentioned in the Constitution. Nevertheless, reasoned Justice Douglas, such a right flows naturally from several of the basic rights which are set down in the first ten Amendments.

He pointed out, for example, that in previous cases the Court had interpreted the First Amendment's protection of the people's right to assemble peaceably as a protection of the "freedom to associate and privacy in one's association." Similarly, Justice Douglas went on, other

99

constitutional guarantees, in addition to those contained in the First Amendment, "create zones of privacy":

> The Third Amendment, in its prohibition against the quartering of soldiers "in any house" in time of peace without the consent of the owner, is another facet of that privacy. The Fourth Amendment explicitly affirms the "right of the people to be secure in their persons, houses, papers, and effects against unreasonable search and seizures." The Fifth Amendment in its Self-Incrimination Clause enables the citizen to create a zone of privacy which government may not force him to surrender to his detriment.

In adopting this line of reasoning, Justice Douglas went beyond the actual wording of the Amendments. He inferred much more than a literal reading could suggest. The "zone of privacy" which he discerned was ample enough to protect those married couples in Connecticut who wished to use contraceptives and persons like Dr. Buxton and Mrs. Griswold who strove to assist them.

"Would we allow the police to search the sacred precincts of marital bedrooms for telltale signs of the use of contraceptives?" asked Justice Douglas. And he promptly answered: "The very idea is repulsive to the notions of privacy surrounding the marriage relationship." He continued:

> We deal with a right of privacy older than the Bill of Rights— older than our political parties, older than our school system. Marriage is a coming together, for better or for worse, hopefully enduring, and intimate to the degree of being sacred. It is an association that promotes a way of life, not causes; a harmony in living, not political faiths; a bilateral loyalty,

THE ZONE OF PRIVACY

not commercial or social projects. Yet it is an association for as noble a purpose as any involved in our prior decisions.

Justice Goldberg, concurring with the majority opinion, found the Ninth Amendment to be applicable to the case at hand. This Amendment states simply that "the enumeration in the Constitution, of certain rights, shall not be construed to deny or disparage others retained by the people." In adding the Amendment, said Justice Goldberg, the authors of the Constitution were making it absolutely clear that they realized that not all of men's fundamental rights had been or could be listed within the first eight Amendments. There were obviously others, not set down, which deserved protection. Privacy in marriage, stressed Justice Goldberg, was one such right:

> The Connecticut statutes here involved deal with a particularly important and sensitive area of privacy—that of the marital relation and the marital home. . . . The fact that no particular provision of the Constitution explicitly forbids the State from disrupting the traditional relation of the family—a relation as old and as fundamental as our entire civilization—surely does not show that the Government was to have the power to do so.

This marked the first time that the Ninth Amendment had been interpreted to fit such a case.

In the opinions of Justice Stewart and Justice Black, the majority was reading into the Constitution a right which was not there. "I like my privacy as well as the next one," commented Justice Black, "but I am nevertheless compelled to admit that Government has a right to invade it unless prohibited by some specific Constitutional provision."

But the ruling of the majority was that the Court could go beyond the literal wording of specific constitutional provisions in judging a law. They recognized that their decision held far-reaching implications. For example, as Justice Goldberg suggested, a law that required compulsory birth control in America would be unconstitutional on the same grounds of "invasion of privacy" as the law which forbade birth control.

If the Justices could find a "right of privacy" in the Constitution, where the word "privacy" was never used, what other "rights" might they not be able to find there? What are the limits on the Court in interpreting the Constitution's language? The Justices could not ignore a problem so basic to the Court's operations. "In determining which rights are fundamental," wrote Justice Goldberg, "judges are not left at large to decide cases in light of their private and personal emotions." Rather, he emphasized, they must look to the traditions and the collective conscience of the people to determine whether a given principle is truly fundamental.

To this, Justice Black replied tartly that "the scientific miracles of this age have not yet produced a gadget which the Court can use to determine what traditions are rooted in the 'collective conscience of our people.' "

There the question rests for the time being—like so many questions of law—unresolved. Statutes on birth control, though not so severe as the one overturned in Connecticut, remain on the books of several states but seem to be lightly observed. It was only in July 1970 that the U.S. Court of Appeals ruled that a Massachusetts law designed to withhold contraceptive devices from *unmarried* persons was in conflict with "fundamental human rights" and therefore unconstitutional.

One may safely predict that the majority's decision in *Griswold v. Connecticut* will be cited in scores of cases still to come, as the Justices try again and again to define that shadowy line between the rights of the individual and the authority of the state. Still, by decisions such as this one, the Warren Court left the area of individual rights larger than it found it.

As Dr. Buxton observed, with more than a touch of sarcasm, after his victory: "It's a great advance for married couples in our state to be able to live a normal life without breaking the law."

Griswold v. Connecticut
1965

BLACK	Dissenting opinion (and joined Stewart)
REED	
FRANKFURTER	
DOUGLAS	OPINION OF COURT
JACKSON	
BURTON	
CLARK	Concurred
MINTON	
WARREN	Concurred (joined Goldberg)
HARLAN	Concurring opinion
BRENNAN	Concurred (joined Goldberg)
WHITTAKER	
STEWART	Dissenting opinion (and joined Black)
WHITE	Concurring opinion
GOLDBERG	Concurring opinion
FORTAS	
MARSHALL	

VI | THE END OF CENSORSHIP

Congress shall make no law . . . abridging the freedom . . . of the press. . . .

In the past decade, official and unofficial censorship of books, movies, and theater in America has been virtually ended. Writers are now free to write about subjects that were strictly forbidden not so long ago; directors are free to stage them and film them. There are no longer any unutterable words.

The reasons for this breakdown of long-existing taboos are many and complicated. Some people, troubled by the development and seeking to place responsibility, have blamed the Supreme Court. There is no doubt that the Court has played a significant role in the process—but its influence has not been either consistent or clear. Like the rest of society, the Court has been trying, without great success, to draw a line between what is permissible in books and films and what is not permissible.

In attempting to pass down rulings for the guidance of police and lower courts on the kinds of materials that are "obscene" and the kinds that are not "obscene," the Court has been faced with exceedingly difficult problems of definition. In 1957 it attempted to meet these problems head-on, with results that satisfied nobody completely—yet did set some guidelines in a murky area. Two cases, decided together, had to do with a New Yorker and a Californian who had been convicted of mailing or selling obscene literature.* The mailing was a federal offense; the selling was a state offense. The question before the Court was whether federal and state obscenity statutes were violations of the provision of the First Amendment that "Congress shall make no law . . . abridging the freedom of speech, or of the press. . . ." That is, the Justices had to decide whether obscene material fell within a constitutionally protected area, where it was safe from restrictive laws.

Reviewing the history of the First Amendment, the majority decided that the Founding Fathers had not intended that obscenity should be protected by the Constitution. The reason for this, in the Court's interpretation, was that the obscene materials, by definition, had no value for the community. As Justice Brennan wrote:

All ideas having even the slightest redeeming social importance—unorthodox ideas, controversial ideas, even ideas hateful to the prevailing climate of opinion—have the full

* *Roth v. United States; Alberts v. California,* 354 U.S. 476 (1957).

protection of the guaranties. . . . But implicit in the history of the First Amendment is the rejection of obscenity as utterly without redeeming social importance.

The convictions, then, were affirmed, but important questions were left unanswered. How, for example, was one to determine whether a work was obscene or not, in the first place? Justice Brennan emphasized in his ruling that a book could not be judged obscene merely because an isolated excerpt might have an undesirable effect on particularly susceptible persons, such as children. Instead, he pointed out that lower courts had been using a more generous test: "whether to the average person, applying contemporary community standards, the dominant theme of the material taken as a whole appeals to prurient interests." And he quoted, approvingly, the instructions to the jury handed down by the judge in the New York case:

The test is not whether it would arouse sexual desires or sexually impure thoughts in those comprising a particular segment of the community, the young, the immature, or the highly prudish, and would leave another segment, the scientific or highly educated or the so-called worldly wise and sophisticated indifferent and unmoved. . . .

The test in each case is the effect of the book, picture, or publication considered as a whole, not upon any particular class, but upon all those whom it is likely to reach. In other words, you determine its impact upon the average person in the community. The books, pictures, and circulars must be judged as a whole, in their entire context, and you are not to consider detached or separate portions in reaching a conclusion. You judge the circulars, pictures, and publications which have been put in evidence by present-day standards of the community. You may ask yourselves does it offend the common conscience of the community by present-day standards. . . .

In this case, ladies and gentlemen of the jury, you and you alone are the exclusive judges of what the common conscience of the community is, and in determining that conscience you are to consider the community as a whole, young and old, educated and uneducated, the religious and the irreligious, men, women, and children.

In dissent from the majority decision in the 1957 cases, Justice Douglas (joined by Justice Black) objected to the fact that, by the majority ruling, punishment could be inflicted merely for the thoughts which obscene material induced in those who encountered it, rather than for any anti-social acts which they might actually perform. He warned:

The test of obscenity the Court endorses today gives the censor free range over a vast domain. To allow the State to step in and punish mere speech or publication that the judge or the jury thinks has an *undesirable* impact on thoughts but that is not shown to be a part of unlawful action is drastically to curtail the First Amendment. . . .

Justices Douglas and Black also objected to the reliance by the Court on "the common conscience of the community." They argued:

Any test that turns on what is offensive to the community's standards is too loose, too capricious, too destructive of freedom of expression to be squared with the First Amendment. Under that test juries can censor, suppress, and punish what they don't like, provided the matter relates to "sexual

THE END OF CENSORSHIP

impurity" or has a tendency "to excite lustful thoughts." This is community censorship in one of its worst forms. . . . If the First Amendment guarantee of freedom of speech and press is to mean anything in this field, it must allow protests even against the moral code that the standard of the day sets for the community. In other words, literature should not be suppressed merely because it offends the moral code of the censor. The legality of a publication in this country should never be allowed to turn either on the purity of thought which it instills in the mind of the reader or on the degree to which it offends the community consciences. By either test, the role of the censor is exalted and society's values in literary freedom are sacrificed.

Justice Douglas warned: "The test that suppresses a cheap tract today can suppress a literary gem tomorrow."

In fact, as it turned out, Justice Douglas's fears were unwarranted. The nation was racing in the direction of far greater permissiveness in what might be printed and filmed than it had ever known. The Justices found themselves not leading but attempting to keep up with fast-moving changes in national attitudes regarding frankness about sex, and they were under heavy pressure to clamp down. As Justice Douglas reported:

Every time an obscenity case is to be argued here, my office is flooded with letters and post cards urging me to protect the community or the Nation by striking down the publication. Their messages are identical, even down to commas and semicolons. The inference is irresistible that they were all copied from a school or church blackboard. Dozens of postal cards often are mailed from the same precinct. The drives are incessant and the pressures are great. Happily we do not bow to them.

The Court's dilemma in attempting to set up certain rules without imposing all-out censorship was apparent in a case decided in 1964.* It concerned the manager of a movie theater in Cleveland Heights, Ohio, who was fined $2,500 for showing a French film, entitled *The Lovers,* in violation of an Ohio obscenity statute. The main objection to the film centered on a few love scenes, which Justice Goldberg found "so fragmentary and fleeting that only a censor's alert would make an audience conscious that something 'questionable' is being portrayed." Justice Brennan reviewed the case:

The Lovers involves a woman bored with her life and marriage who abandons her husband and family for a young archaeologist with whom she has suddenly fallen in love. There is an explicit love scene in the last reel of the film, and the State's objections are based almost entirely upon that scene. The film was favorably reviewed in a number of national publications, though disparaged in others, and was rated by at least two critics of national stature among the best films of the year in which it was produced.

The Court reversed the conviction. Recalling the rule spelled out in the *Roth* case—which left the judgment of whether a book or film is obscene, "to the average person, applying contemporary community standards"— Justice Brennan pointed out that even though *The Lovers* might be considered undesirable for children, it could not on that ground alone be suppressed. He sug-

* *Jacobellis v. Ohio,* 378 U.S. 184 (1964).

gested that state and local authorities might consider passing laws directed specifically at preventing certain types of material from reaching children rather than banning the material altogether. (It was not long after this decision that the movie industry established its system of rating films according to their suitability for minors.)

The victory of *The Lovers,* along with the Supreme Court's overturning of state bans on the sale of controversial books, dismayed many clergymen. A group of nine conservative ministers, priests, and rabbis issued a statement that charged the Court with setting "degeneracy as the standard way of American life." They wrote:

In finding that the Constitution was intended as a guarantee for the dissemination of filth, and a device to deprive the public of the right to protect itself against vile and corrupting publications, the "under God" foundations of the United States were implied to be irrelevant.

These decisions cannot be accepted quietly by the American people if this nation is to survive. Giving free rein to the vile depiction of violence, perversion, illicit sex, and, in consequence, to their performance, is an unerring sign of progressive decay and decline. . . . We urge that religious leaders of all faiths in all communities stand together in vociferously decrying the fact that the Court has presumed to recast the moral law.

But despite such protests, the national current was moving strongly against censorship.

Two conclusions could be drawn from the Court's obscenity decisions over the years. The first was that it was not possible to define the word "obscenity" in any way that would end legal controversy once and for all; that depended on the reaction of each individual to the controversial material, and individual reactions differ greatly. The second conclusion was that the Court's judgments were part of a larger social change: old barriers were being overthrown, and all the Court could hope to do was keep the change moving within set speed limits, rather than stop it altogether.

As Justice Warren stated the challenge in his dissent in the case of *The Lovers:* "No government . . . should be forced to choose between repressing all material, including that within the realm of decency, and allowing unrestrained license to publish any material, no matter how vile."

The Court's difficulties in establishing workable guidelines was made clear to the nation on March 21, 1966, when it handed down three quite different rulings in obscenity cases.

It reversed the prohibition by the State of Massachusetts of the eighteenth-century English novel, *Fanny Hill,* a classic of pornography.* The grounds for this decision were those laid down in 1957 that no book could be prohibited unless it were *"utterly* without redeeming social value."

Responding to Justice Clark's dissent ("Though I am not known to be a purist—or a shrinking violet—this book is too much even for me"), Justice Douglas emphasized:

---

* *A Book Named "John Cleland's Memoirs of a Woman of Pleasure" v. Attorney General of Massachusetts,* 383 U.S. 413 (1966).

THE END OF CENSORSHIP

We are judges, not literary experts, or historians, or philosophers. We are not competent to render an independent judgment as to the worth of this or any other book, except in our capacity as private citizens. . . . If there is to be censorship, the wisdom of experts on such matters as literary merit and historical significance must be evaluated.

(Numerous critics had testified that *Fanny Hill* had value as a work of literature.)

In a second case, the Court confirmed, over the objections of Justices Douglas, Black, and Stewart, the conviction in New York of a bookseller for publishing obscene books.* Whereas most of the Justices found the material in this case clearly obscene by its own criteria, Justice Black criticized what he called "the un-American policy of censoring the thoughts and opinions of people" and reiterated his objections to having the Court saddled with "deciding on a case-by-case, sight-by-sight personal judgment of the members of this Court what pornography (whatever that means) is too hard-core for people to see or read."

And in the third case, while confirming the conviction in Pennsylvania of the publisher of three allegedly obscene publications, the Court laid down a new rule for determining what constitutes "obscenity" under the law.† Once again it fell to Justice Brennan to deliver the majority opinion—an opinion that startled many close observers of the Court.

Evidently the Justices had been troubled by the fact

---

* *Mishkin v. New York,* 383 U.S. 502 (1966).
† *Ginzburg v. United States,* 383 U.S. 463 (1966).

that so few of the many works of alleged pornography they were compelled to read seemed to be censorable under the guidelines set up by the 1957 decision. Now, in analyzing the publications in question in this 1966 case, the majority put its emphasis not on what actually appeared in the publications' pages but on the way in which they had been advertised to the public. The advertisements had apparently been devised to appeal to customers desiring pornographic material, and it was for this reason that the Court confirmed the conviction of the publisher, Ralph Ginzburg, who had been given a sentence of five years in prison and fined $28,000.

Liberal publications, usually friendly to the Court, were appalled at the decision. "Mr. Ginzburg's sentence is an outrage," declared the *New Republic,* adding, "There is little if anything to be said for Justice Brennan's opinion, or for the majority decision in the *Ginzburg* case."

There were four separate dissents from this decision —from Justices Black, Douglas, Harlan, and Stewart. Expressing his shock at the notion of sending anyone to prison for publishing anything, Justice Douglas protested:

The advertisements of our best magazines are chock-full of thighs, ankles, calves, bosoms, eyes, and hair to draw the potential buyer's attention to lotions, tires, food, liquor, clothing, autos, and even insurance policies. The sexy ad neither adds nor detracts from the quality of the merchandise being offered for sale. And I do not see how it adds to or detracts one whit from the legality of the book being distributed. A book should stand on its own, irrespective of the reasons why it was written or the wiles used in selling it.

... the First Amendment allows all ideas to be expressed—whether orthodox, popular, offbeat, or repulsive. I do not think it permissible to draw lines between the "good" and the "bad" and be true to the Constitutional mandate to let all ideas alone. ... under our Charter all regulation or control of expression is banned. Government does not sit to reveal where the "truth" is. People are left to pick and choose between competing offerings. ... The theory is that people are mature enough to pick and choose, to recognize trash when they see it, to be attracted to the literature that satisfies their deepest need, and, hopefully, to move from plateau to plateau and finally reach the world of enduring ideas. I think this is the ideal of the Free Society written into our Constitution.

Justice Harlan observed that the new advertising test was entirely unrelated to the language, purposes, or history of the federal law being applied, and it was also different from the test used by the lower court to convict the publisher. He criticized the majority decision as an "astonishing piece of judicial improvisation."

Justice Black concluded that, on the basis of the day's conflicting opinions, "no person, not even the most learned judge, much less a layman, is capable of knowing in advance whether certain material comes within the area of 'obscenity' as that term is confused by the Court today." He added: "I think the First Amendment forbids any kind or type or nature of governmental censorship over views as distinguished from conduct."

With this, Justice Stewart agreed wholeheartedly. He wrote:

Censorship reflects a society's lack of confidence in itself. It is a hallmark of an authoritarian regime. Long ago those who wrote our First Amendment charted a different course. They believed a society can be truly strong only when it is truly free. In the realm of expression they put their faith, for better or for worse, in the enlightened choice of the people, free from the interference of a policeman's intrusive thumb or a judge's heavy hand. So it is that the Constitution protects coarse expression as well as refined, and vulgarity no less than elegance. A book worthless to me may convey something of value to my neighbor. In the free society to which our Constitution has committed us, it is for each to choose for himself. . . .

As it has turned out, the Court's effort to apply the touch of a brake to the nation's rush to overthrow long-standing prohibitions had little effect. The movement, which the Court itself had helped to get going, toward open expression in the once-closed area of sex has proved too strong. Today the kind of publications put out by the convicted Ralph Ginzburg seem mild in comparison to what can be found in bookstores and seen in theaters throughout the land.

	Roth v. U.S. 1957	Jacobellis v. Ohio 1964
BLACK	Dissented (joined Douglas)	Concurring opinion
REED		
FRANKFURTER	Concurred	
DOUGLAS	Dissenting opinion	Concurred (joined Black)
JACKSON		
BURTON	Concurred	
CLARK	Concurred	Dissented (joined Warren)
MINTON		
WARREN	Concurring opinion	Dissenting opinion
HARLAN	Opinion concurring in part, dissenting in part	Dissenting opinion
BRENNAN	OPINION OF COURT	OPINION OF COURT
WHITTAKER	Concurred	
STEWART		Concurring opinion
WHITE		Concurred
GOLDBERG		Concurring opinion (and joined Brennan)
FORTAS		
MARSHALL		

"Memoirs" v. Mass. 1966	Mishkin v. New York 1966	Ginzburg v. U.S. 1966
Concurred	Dissenting opinion	Dissenting opinion
Concurring opinion	Dissented	Dissenting opinion
Dissenting opinion	Concurred	Concurred
Concurred (joined Brennan)	Concurred	Concurred
Dissenting opinion	Concurred (joined Brennan)	Dissenting opinion
OPINION OF COURT	OPINION OF COURT	OPINION OF COURT
Concurred	Dissenting opinion	Dissenting opinion
Dissenting opinion	Concurred	Concurred
Concurred (joined Brennan)	Concurred	Concurred

VII | THE RIGHT TO BE UNPOPULAR

> *Congress shall make no law . . . abridging . . . the right of the people peaceably to assemble. . . .*

There are few countries in the world where a political dissenter has as much freedom to speak out against the government and its institutions as in America. That is one of our proudest claims. Yet often in our history, people with unpopular opinions have become targets of federal and state officials who sought to curtail their rights.

After the end of World War II, the main targets of such actions were American Communists. They were thought by many to be threats to the national security, to be "subversive," and efforts were made to keep them from taking jobs in government and in certain industries, from traveling to other countries, and from teaching in the public schools.

Cases involving the rights of Communists began to reach the Court in the 1950's—a decade when the Cold War between the Soviet Union and the United States was raging and when anti-Communist feelings ran high in this country. The Court's decisions in these early cases were not entirely consistent and satisfied neither those who were leading the anti-Communist crusade nor those who championed Communists' civil liberties.

In the 1960's, however, the Court made a number of rulings which, taken together, added up to the principle that an individual could not be deprived of such basic rights as a job or a passport because he was a member of the Communist Party. The decisions reviewed below show the reasoning of the Justices as they weighed the requirements of national security against the rights of individuals.

Under a civil-service law passed in New York State in 1939, members of any organization that advocated the overthrow of the government by force or violence were prohibited from teaching in the public schools. In 1949 this ruling was implemented by another law, called the Feinberg Law; it required the New York State Board of Regents, which administers New York's schools, to draw up a list of banned organizations and to make membership in any of them sufficient evidence to disqualify a person from holding a teaching post.

In 1952, two years before Earl Warren's appointment as Chief Justice, this law was upheld by the Supreme

Court.* In delivering the majority opinion, Justice Sherman Minton stated:

> It is the purpose of the Feinberg Law to provide for the disqualification and removal of superintendents of schools, teachers, and employees in the public schools in any city or school district of the State who advocate the overthrow of the government by unlawful means or who are members of organizations which have a like purpose.

He then asked whether such a rule abridged the freedom of speech and assembly of people who wanted to work in the public-school system—and replied that it did not:

> It is clear that such persons have the right under our law to assemble, speak, think, and believe as they will . . . it is equally clear that they have no right to work for the State in the school system on their own terms. . . . They may work for the school system upon the reasonable terms laid down by the proper authorities of New York. If they do not choose to work on such terms, they are at liberty to retain their beliefs and associations and go elsewhere. Has the State thus deprived them of any right to free speech or assembly? We think not.

Justice Minton summed up his views:

> A teacher works in a sensitive area in a schoolroom. There he shapes the attitudes of young minds toward the society in which they live. In this, the State has a vital concern. It must preserve the integrity of the schools. That the school authorities have the right and the duty to screen the officials, teachers, and employees as to their fitness to maintain the

---

* *Adler v. Board of Education,* 342 U.S. 485 (1952).

integrity of the schools as a part of ordered society cannot be doubted.

This line of reasoning was hotly protested by Justices Black and Douglas. Justice Black argued that the Feinberg Law made it dangerous for schoolteachers "to think or say anything except what a transient majority happen to approve of at the moment."

Justice Douglas warned that the rule of "guilt by association" would make teachers fearful and threaten freedom of discussion in the classrooms. So long as the teacher is a law-abiding citizen, held Justice Douglas, "so long as her performance within the public-school system meets professional standards, her private life, her political philosophy, her social creed should not be the cause of reprisals against her."

It would be the mid-1960's before the minority views of Justices Douglas and Black became the majority opinion of the Supreme Court. By then, of course, the membership of the Court had changed significantly and the nation's anxiety regarding Communists was no longer at quite so high a pitch.

The Court's change of heart was clearly expressed in 1966, in a case involving a young Quaker couple, Vernon and Barbara Elfbrandt, who taught junior high school in Tucson, Arizona. The Elfbrandts had refused to sign a loyalty oath under a newly enacted state law. They were not Communists and were willing to pledge allegiance to the state and the nation but objected on principle to having to sign an oath that they were not members of any group that had as "one of its purposes ... the overthrow of the Government."

The Elfbrandts continued to teach—without pay—as their case went through the courts. For five years they were supported by loans and gifts from friends and sympathetic strangers. Finally, in 1966, the high Court ruled 5 to 4 in their favor—which meant $60,000 in back pay for the Elfbrandts.* The oath they had refused to sign, wrote Justice Douglas for the majority, was unconstitutional, since it punished a person merely for his membership in a given group, even if he did not share all the aims of that group.

Ruled the Court: "Those who join an organization but do not share its unlawful purposes and who do not participate in its unlawful activities surely pose no threat, either as citizens or as public employees." In the majority opinion, the Arizona loyalty oath rested on "guilt by association" and infringed the individual's freedoms under the Constitution.

Obviously, the majority view in 1966 was very different from what it had been in 1952, and a year later the Court found an opportunity to reverse flatly its earlier approval of New York's Feinberg Law. This case began in 1962, when the University of Buffalo was made part of the State University of New York, and all staff members were required to sign "Feinberg certificates."

* *Elfbrandt v. Russell,* 384 U.S. 11 (1966).

Four staff members refused to sign the certificates and so were faced with dismissal. They went to the courts with a challenge to the constitutionality of the Feinberg Law. When the law was upheld in federal district court, they appealed to the Supreme Court.*

The majority opinion was delivered by Justice Brennan, who had not been on the Court in 1952. He acknowledged that the state had an "interest in protecting its educational system from subversion," but criticized the Feinberg Law for its vague language, which could be interpreted to cover "mere expression of belief," and observed that "it would be a brave teacher who would not stay as far as possible from utterance or acts which might jeopardize his living. . . ."

Restating the rule laid down by the Court in the previous year's *Elfbrandt* case, Justice Brennan declared that a person could not be prohibited from holding a teaching post with the state on the basis of membership alone, "without a specific intent to further the unlawful aims of an organization."

This decision marked what Justice Clark, speaking heatedly for the four-man minority (he was joined by Justices Harlan, Stewart, and White), called a "death blow" for the Feinberg Law, which had once been upheld as constitutional by the Court. In Justice Clark's opinion, the majority had "swept away one of our most precious rights, namely, the right of self-preservation." As Justice Clark saw the issue, it was a narrow one:

---

* *Keyishian v. Board of Regents of the State University of New York,* 385 U.S. 589 (1967).

May the State provide that one who, after a hearing with full judicial review, is found to willfully and deliberately advocate, advise, or teach that our Government should be overthrown by force, violence, or other unlawful means . . . is disqualified from teaching in its university? My answer, in keeping with all of our cases up until today, is "Yes!"

But, declared Justice Brennan, in words that were reminiscent of the dissent of Justice Douglas fifteen years before:

Our Nation is deeply committed to safeguarding academic freedom, which is of transcendent value to all of us and not merely to the teachers concerned. That freedom is therefore a special concern of the First Amendment, which does not tolerate laws that cast a pall of orthodoxy over the classroom.

Whether or not the teachers involved in these loyalty-oath cases were actually Communists was not at issue. Even if they had been, however, the principles on which the Court's majority based its decision would have remained the same. This was demonstrated in a case decided in 1964, when two prominent leaders of the Communist Party who had had their passports revoked by the U.S. Department of State appealed their case to the Supreme Court.*

In taking away the Communists' passports, State Department officials were carrying out a provision of a law (the Subversive Activities Control Act) that made it illegal for any member of the Communist Party to apply for a passport or to use one. Both the appellants in this case—Elizabeth Gurley Flynn, the Communist

* *Aptheker v. Secretary of State,* 378 U.S. 500 (1964).

Party chairman, and Herbert Aptheker, editor of the party journal, *Political Affairs*—were native-born Americans who had held valid passports before the law took effect.

Speaking for the majority, Justice Goldberg emphasized the broad scope of the section of the law that was being challenged: First, it applied to all members of the Communist Party, whether or not they fully shared all the ideas of the organization, and regardless of the degree of their commitment, knowledge, or activity. Second, the law covered all travel, regardless of its purpose; even visiting a sick relative abroad was forbidden. Third, the law covered all areas of the world, not just areas that were considered sensitive because of national security.

In light of these facts, the majority found that the law was unconstitutional because it swept too widely across the guarantees of the Fifth Amendment. Freedom of travel, declared Justice Goldberg, "is a constitutional liberty closely related to rights of free speech and association." To this, Justice Douglas, in a concurring opinion, added:

Free movement by the citizen is of course as dangerous to a tyrant as free expression of ideas or the rights of assembly, and it is therefore controlled in most countries in the interests of security. That is why riding in boxcars carries extreme penalties in Communist lands. That is why the ticketing of people and the use of identification papers are routine matters under totalitarian regimes, yet abhorrent in the United States.

Justices Clark, Harlan, and White dissented from the decision. "The right to travel," stressed Justice Clark, "is not absolute." Responding to Justice Goldberg's attack on the broad scope of the Subversive Activities Control Act, he pointed out that there was no doubt Herbert Aptheker and Elizabeth Gurley Flynn were committed to the Communist Party and that the Congress had evidence that Communists had used passports to engage in subversive activities against this country.

This evidence afforded the Congress a rational basis upon which to place the denial of passports to members of the Communist Party in the United States. The denial is reasonably related to the national security. The degree of restraint upon travel is outweighed by the dangers to our very existence.

But the majority felt that there was a higher issue at stake here. As Justice Black wrote:

This case offers another appropriate occasion to point out that the Framers thought (and I agree) that the best way to promote the internal security of our people is to protect their First Amendment freedoms of speech, press, religion, and assembly, and that we cannot take away the liberty of groups whose views most people detest without jeopardizing the liberty of all others whose views, though popular today, may themselves be detested tomorrow.

Adler v. Board of Education
1952

BLACK	Dissenting opinion (and joined Douglas)
REED	Concurred
FRANKFURTER	Dissenting opinion
DOUGLAS	Dissenting opinion
JACKSON	Concurred
BURTON	Concurred
CLARK	Concurred
MINTON	OPINION OF COURT
WARREN	
HARLAN	
BRENNAN	
WHITTAKER	
STEWART	
WHITE	
GOLDBERG	
FORTAS	
MARSHALL	

Justice Vinson also concurred

Elfbrandt v. Russell 1966	Keyishian v. State University 1967	Aptheker v. Secretary of State 1964
Concurred	Concurred	Concurred
OPINION OF COURT	Concurred	Concurred
Dissented (joined White)	Dissenting opinion	Dissenting opinion
Concurred	Concurred	Concurred
Dissented (joined White)	Dissented (joined Clark)	Dissented (joined Clark)
Concurred	OPINION OF COURT	Concurred
Dissented (joined White)	Dissented (joined Clark)	Concurred
Dissenting opinion	Dissented (joined Clark)	Dissented (joined Clark in part)
		OPINION OF COURT
Concurred	Concurred	

VIII | ONE MAN—ONE VOTE

No State shall . . . deny to any person within its jurisdiction the equal protection of the laws.

From its beginnings, America has been a nation on the move, families in search of a better life. For the first century of our existence, the movement was westward, as pioneers and settlers transformed a wilderness into farms and pastureland and new towns. This century has seen the astounding growth of America's cities. In the 1940's and 1950's, the cities attracted many families who were finding it difficult to make a decent living in rural areas; new machines had greatly increased farm productivity but had reduced the need for manpower. So the population of our cities and the suburbs around them soared, while that of rural areas remained static or actually decreased. Whereas in 1900 six out of ten Americans lived in rural areas, by 1960 seven out of ten lived in or near cities.

One direct consequence of this great population shift was that the make-up of Congress and the state legislatures became unrepresentative. Having been organized in the days when most people lived on or around farms, these bodies now tended to give too much voting power to the minority in rural areas and too little to the majority in the big cities and new suburbs. Since any change to adjust to the new reality of where people actually lived would have meant a loss of political power by entrenched officeholders, few changes were made.

The results of this lag were plain to see. In the 1940's, the legislatures of more than forty states could be elected by a minority of the voters. In a state like Connecticut, whose legislature had been established in Colonial times, barely 12 per cent of the voters could control the state House of Representatives. The little town of Union, Connecticut (population, 400), was entitled to as many representatives as the big city of Hartford (population, 162,000). Nor was Connecticut unique. Burlington, the largest city in Vermont (population, 35,000), was entitled to one state senator, as was the hamlet of Victory (population, 46). The more than 6 million residents of Los Angeles County had the same representation in the California State Senate as barely 15,000 people in sparsely populated communities. In Michigan, there was one congressional district that contained 800,000 people and another that contained fewer than 200,000; each sent one Congressman to Washington. Thus, four city dwellers in the big district had the same representation as a single voter in the rural district.

ONE MAN—ONE VOTE

The unfair apportionment of seats in the national and state legislatures was a source of concern and irritation to city dwellers through much of the 1950's, and attempts were made to get the Supreme Court to rule on the inequity. But the Court had shown itself reluctant to go into the matter. In 1946 a decision written by Justice Frankfurter held that the Court did not have the power to force the Illinois legislature to redistrict that state's congressional districts, even though they ranged in size from 112,116 people to 914,053 people.* Over the dissent of Justices Black, Douglas, and Murphy, Justice Frankfurter ruled that in a "political" matter of this sort, it was up to the state legislatures themselves to correct any unfairness. But, in fact, years passed and the unfairness, far from being corrected, grew steadily worse.

In 1959 a group of residents of Memphis, Tennessee, brought an action before a three-judge federal court. According to the Mayor of Nashville, another large Tennessee city, "the pigs and chickens in our smaller counties have better representation in the Tennessee legislature than the people of Nashville." The judges expressed sympathy for the complaint that in Tennessee about one-third of the voters could elect about two-thirds of the state Assembly; they acknowledged that despite a fivefold increase in the number of voters and significant population shifts, the Assembly had not been redistricted since 1901: "The evil is a serious one which

* *Colegrove v. Green,* 328 U.S. 549 (1946).

should be corrected without delay." But in light of the high Court's 1946 decision, the judges concluded that they simply lacked the power to do anything about the matter: "There are indeed some rights guaranteed by the Constitution for the violations of which the courts cannot give redress. . . ." And they rejected the suit. The Memphis group, joined by the cities of Knoxville and Chattanooga and the Mayor of Nashville, appealed to the Supreme Court.

This time the Court, whose composition had changed markedly since the 1946 decision, ruled that the city voters did have a complaint suitable for the courts because their rights under the Equal Protection Clause of the Fourteenth Amendment were being violated; they sent the case back to the lower court for a ruling.*

Justices Frankfurter and Harlan dissented strongly from the majority opinion written by Justice Brennan. The dissenters granted that the Tennessee legislature did not fairly represent the state's voters. But in their view, as Justice Frankfurter put it, the case was not subject to supervision by the courts. Justices Frankfurter and Harlan called for the "wise exercise of self-restraint and discipline" on the part of their fellow Justices. They argued that it was not in the power of the federal courts to interfere in any state's political arrangements, however unwise or undesirable. If the Court interfered, they warned, its prestige would suffer.

The feelings of the majority were most forcibly ex-

* *Baker v. Carr,* 369 U.S. 186 (1962).

pressed in a concurring opinion written by Justice Clark. Noting that a Tennessee county with about 2,000 residents was entitled to the same number of representatives as a county of 25,000, Justice Clark declared that only one conclusion was possible: "Tennessee's apportionment is a crazy quilt without any rational basis," and the state "is guilty of a clear violation of the state constitution and of the [federal] rights of the plaintiffs."

Replying to the argument of Justices Frankfurter and Harlan that the place for voters to seek redress was the state legislature itself, Justice Clark noted that those in control of the legislature refused to make any changes because it would mean a loss of personal power:

The majority of the voters have been caught up in a legislative strait jacket. . . . The people have been rebuffed at the hands of the Assembly; they have tried the constitutional convention route, but since the call must originate in the Assembly, that, too, has been fruitless. They have tried the Tennessee courts with the same results, and the Governors have fought the tide only to flounder. . . . We therefore must conclude that the people of Tennessee are stymied and without judicial intervention will be saddled with the present discrimination in the affairs of their State Government.

Declared Justice Clark: "The Court's decision today supports the proposition for which our forebears fought and many died, namely, that . . . the form of Government must be representative. That is the keystone upon which our Government was founded and lacking which no republic can survive."

In the wake of this key decision, and despite criticisms by thoughtful observers that it would "weaken the complex American system for diffusing power and protecting minorities," efforts got under way in most states to reapportion their legislatures and bring them into line with where voters actually lived. However, since the Supreme Court had so far only laid down the principle that federal courts had jurisdiction in the field, but had not actually set any standard for apportionment, there was considerable confusion. This was a new area, and the lower courts had no precedent to guide them. In 1963 the high Court returned to the subject and did lay down a standard, which at once became known as "One Man—One Vote."

The case this time originated with voters in Fulton County, Georgia—the largest county in the state*— who filed their suit just seventy-seven minutes after hearing the decision in the Tennessee case. They were objecting to the system used for counting votes in the Georgia Democratic primary for U.S. Senator and for statewide offices. In most Southern states, victory in Democratic Party primaries was virtually equivalent to election. Here, too, small counties were grossly favored over large ones—by as much as 14 to 1.

The voice of Justice Douglas, who had opposed the 1946 decision, now became the majority. Over Justice Harlan's lone dissent (Justice Frankfurter having recently retired from the bench), Justice Douglas laid down this rule:

* *Gray v. Sanders,* 372 U.S. 368 (1963).

ONE MAN—ONE VOTE

Once the geographical unit for which a representative is to be chosen is designated, all who participate in the election are to have an equal vote—whatever their race, whatever their sex, whatever their occupation, whatever their income, and wherever their home may be in that geographical unit.

The conception of political equality from the Declaration of Independence to Lincoln's Gettysburg Address, to the Fifteenth, Seventeenth, and Nineteenth Amendments can mean only one thing—one person, one vote.

So now the standard was established. Still, the problem remained of applying it around the country—a problem that occupied many courts in many places in the months that followed, as state legislatures set to work on various reapportionment schemes. In 1964 the Supreme Court itself delivered two more major rulings that helped make effective the principles it had already laid down. One involved the election of Congressmen, the other the election of state legislators.

Justice Black delivered the Court's opinion in the first case. It was brought by an Atlanta accountant and three local lawyers who complained that, because their congressional district was more than twice the size of the average district in Georgia, they were being deprived of the full value of their right to vote. The Court agreed, ruling that the command of Article I, Section 2, of the U.S. Constitution that Representatives to Congress be chosen "by the people of the several states" means that "as nearly as practicable one man's vote in a Congressional election is to be worth as much as another's."*

* *Wesberry v. Sanders,* 376 U.S. 1 (1964).

Wrote Justice Black:

> To say that a vote is worth more in one district than in another would not only run counter to our fundamental ideas of democratic government, it would cast aside the principle of a House of Representatives elected "by the People," a principle tenaciously fought for and established at the Constitutional Convention. . . . No right is more precious in a free country than that of having a voice in the election of those who make the laws under which, as good citizens, we must live. Other rights, even the most basic, are illusory if the right to vote is undermined.

Still in the minority, Justice Harlan, who held a strict view of the Court's powers to invervene in "political" matters, took issue with the majority's interpretation of Article I, Section 2, and of Justice Black's reading of the debates at the Constitutional Convention. It not infrequently happens that Justices, analyzing the same historical material, will come to quite different conclusions as to its meaning for the present day, and that was so in this case.

Justice Harlan expressed his astonishment at "a decision which casts grave doubt on the constitutionality of the composition of the House of Representatives . . . [and] places in jeopardy the seats of almost all the members of the present House of Representatives." He criticized his colleagues for attempting to make reforms in a field which, under the Constitution, was left "exclusively" to the political process. In a statement that summed up his philosophy of judicial restraint, which has a long and honorable history, Justice Harlan wrote:

ONE MAN—ONE VOTE

This Court, no less than all other branches of the Government, is bound by the Constitution. The Constitution does not confer on the Court blanket authority to step into every situation where the political branch may be thought to have fallen short. The stability of this institution ultimately depends not only upon its being alert to keep the other branches of Government within constitutional bounds but equally upon recognition of the limitations on the Court's own functions in the constitutional system. What is done today saps the political process.

In the *Wesberry v. Sanders* case, Justice Harlan was joined by Justice Stewart in his dissent, and Justice Clark wrote an opinion that concurred in part and dissented in part; but in the second major reapportionment case of 1964, Justice Harlan again stood alone.

The complaining voter here, an Alabama man, had won in a lower court when he showed that his county, with a population of more than 600,000, and another county, with a population of around 15,000, were each entitled to a single state senator. Alabama had not done any substantial reapportionment for sixty years— during which time its population had doubled and its cities had grown. The state appealed the case to the Supreme Court.* (Similar cases originated in New York, Maryland, Virginia, Delaware, and Colorado.)

In his dissent, Justice Harlan once again tried to make clear his concept of the limits which the Constitution placed on the powers of the Supreme Court and the dangers of exceeding those limits. The Court, he in-

---

* *Reynolds v. Sims*, 377 U.S. 533 (1964).

sisted, had only the power of interpreting the Constitution, not of altering it; that was a job for the nation's voters. He wrote:

> . . . These decisions give support to a current mistaken view of the Constitution and the constitutional function of the Court. This view, in a nutshell, is that every major social ill in this country can find its cure in some constitutional "principle," and that this Court should "take the lead" in promoting reform when other branches of Government fail to act. The Constitution is not a panacea for every blot upon the public welfare nor should this Court, ordained as a judicial body, be thought of as a general haven for reform movements. The Constitution is an instrument of government, fundamental to which is the premise that in a diffusion of governmental authority lies the greatest promise that this Nation will realize liberty for all its citizens. This Court, limited in function in accordance with that premise, does not serve its high purpose when it exceeds its authority, even to satisfy justified impatience with the slow workings of the political process. For when, in the name of constitutional interpretation, the Court *adds* something to the Constitution that was deliberately excluded from it, the Court in reality substitutes its view of what should be so for the amending process.

This was an important argument, basic to the operations of the Supreme Court. As Justice Louis D. Brandeis said years before, "The most important thing we do, is not doing." But, for the majority in this case, the issue was clear: voters in many states were being deprived of their full constitutional right to elect their representatives and it was the obligation of the Court to uphold this right. "Judicial restraint" was not the philosophy that guided the Warren Court.

"Legislators represent people, not trees or acres," declared the Chief Justice in his decision in this case. He pointed out that in effect, under existing apportionment schemes, the votes of people in small counties were worth twice as much or five times as much or even ten times as much as the votes of people in large counties, and this was a violation of the Constitution.

Critics were quick to recall that Earl Warren had written in 1948, when he was Governor of California: "Many California counties are far more important in the life of the State than their population bears to the entire population of the State. It is for this reason that I have never been in favor of restricting the representation in the State Senate to a strictly population basis."

But times change, and so evidently do the opinions even of Chief Justices of the Supreme Court. In 1964 Justice Warren emphasized:

> To the extent that a citizen's right to vote is debased, he is that much less a citizen. The fact that an individual lives here or there is not a legitimate reason for overweighting or diluting the efficacy of his vote. The complexions of societies and civilizations change, often with amazing rapidity. A nation once primarily rural in character becomes predominantly urban. Representation schemes once fair and equitable become archaic and outdated. But the basic principle of representative government remains, and must remain, unchanged—the weight of a citizen's vote cannot be made to depend on where he lives.

A few years later, he would select this set of rulings as the most important of his term on the Supreme Court.

The apportionment decisions of the Court—later expanded to cover local as well as statewide elections—aroused a great furor among legislators in state capitals as well as in Washington. Whereas Attorney General Robert F. Kennedy called the Court's ruling "a landmark in the development of representative government," Senator Richard B. Russell of Georgia called it "another major assault on our constitutional system." Dozens of bills were put forward in Congress that would have curbed the Court's powers in this area, and the House of Representatives actually passed a bill in 1964 that would have taken away from federal courts the authority in redistricting cases which they had so recently assumed. But the bill did not pass the Senate, and in time the debate died down as state legislatures around the country got on with the job of revising their election procedures to approach the single standard set by the Supreme Court: One Person—One Vote.

	Colegrove v. Green 1946	Baker v. Carr 1962
BLACK	Dissenting opinion	Concurred
REED	Concurred (joined Frankfurter)	
FRANKFURTER	OPINION OF COURT	Dissenting opinion (and joined Harlan)
DOUGLAS	Dissented (joined Black)	Concurring opinion
JACKSON	Concurred	
BURTON	Concurred (joined Frankfurter)	
CLARK		Concurring opinion
MINTON		
WARREN		Concurred
HARLAN		Dissenting opinion (and joined Frankfurter)
BRENNAN		OPINION OF COURT
WHITTAKER		Did not participate
STEWART		Concurring opinion
WHITE		
GOLDBERG		
FORTAS		
MARSHALL		

Justice Rutledge wrote a concurring opinion and Justice Stone also concurred. Justice Murphy dissented

Gray v. Sanders 1963	Wesberry v. Sanders 1964	Reynolds v. Sims 1964
Concurred	OPINION OF COURT	Concurred
OPINION OF COURT	Concurred	Concurred
Concurred (joined Stewart)	Opinion concurring in part, dissenting in part	Concurring opinion
Concurred	Concurred	OPINION OF COURT
Dissenting opinion	Dissenting opinion	Dissenting opinion
Concurred	Concurred	Concurred
Concurring opinion	Dissenting opinion (joined Harlan in part)	Concurring opinion
Concurred	Concurred	Concurred
Concurred	Concurred	Concurred

IX | MILK FOR CHILDREN

> *No State shall . . . deny to any person within its jurisdiction the equal protection of the laws.*

In October 1966 Mrs. Sylvester Smith, once widowed, once deserted, thirty-four years old, and black, was notified by the Department of Pensions and Security of Dallas County, Alabama, that it was cutting off payments to her family under the Aid to Dependent Children program. This meant a loss of about twenty-nine dollars a month, more than one-quarter of the Smith household income. It also signaled the beginning of a momentous test, resolved by the Supreme Court nearly two years later, of a state's power to deprive children of aid to which they are entitled by a federal welfare program.

At a time when the government's entire approach to the poor was coming under radical criticism, the Court delivered a blow to state authorities, Northern as well as

Southern, who had been withholding federal dollars from residents because of race, sexual activity, or other matters irrelevant to their need. The *Smith* decision, which affected more than 21,000 children in Alabama and perhaps as many as 400,000 throughout the country, was the first handed down by the high Court in a dispute over public welfare. Like Linda Brown, the schoolgirl from Topeka who won the 1954 school-integration decision, and Clarence Earl Gideon, the Florida convict whose right to an attorney was upheld in 1963, Mrs. Sylvester Smith set in motion a dramatic change in American society.

In first giving aid to Mrs. Smith and then taking it away, Alabama was acting as an agent of the federal government, which set up the Aid to Dependent Children program (ADC) under the Social Security Act. Family payments vary according to need and number of children. In Alabama they averaged about fifteen dollars a child each month—about half the established level of "need." Most of this was contributed by the federal government.

Designed to help children who have been deprived of a parent by death, incapacity, or simply by "continued absence from the home," ADC has for years been under attack from those who see it as an inducement to immoral behavior, especially among minority groups. "By taxing the good people to pay for these programs," said Governor Orval Faubus of Arkansas (remembered for his role in attempting to bar black children from his state's schools), "we are putting a premium on illegitimacy never before known in the world."

Mrs. Smith's children met all the original requirements for aid, but they did not qualify under one regulation that Alabama, along with twenty other states, had added. The Smith children were ruled ineligible because their mother was thought to be maintaining a continuing sexual relationship with a "substitute father"—who, presumably, was expected to help support the children.

Mrs. Smith first applied for ADC in March 1956, a few months after the death of her husband. She was twenty-three years old and was left with three children—Ida Elizabeth, three; Ernestine, two; and Willie Lewis, six months. Aid was granted. In January 1957 she had a fourth child, Willie James, the son of one Lois Fuller. Willie James was added to the ADC lists in June 1963, after Fuller disappeared. The family received about sixty-seven dollars a month until March 1966, when Ida Elizabeth, thirteen years old and unmarried, bore a daughter of her own and was scratched from the budget.

That summer Mrs. Smith moved with her daughters and baby granddaughter from the country town of Tyler up to Selma, where she had found a job as a cook and waitress in a cafe—3:30 A.M. to noon for sixteen dollars a week, later raised to twenty dollars. Her two sons stayed in the country with their grandparents, and joined the family in Selma on weekends.

One result of this move was that the Smiths were assigned to a new caseworker, Mrs. Jacquelyn Stancil. After reviewing the Smith records and noting mention there of one William E. Williams, Mrs. Stancil questioned a third party and was told that Mrs. Smith was receiving weekend visits from Williams, who still lived in Tyler, fifteen miles south of Selma. "When I asked who told," recalled Mrs. Smith, "she said, 'It was a little bird.' I'd like to meet that little bird."

In September 1966 Mrs. Stancil notified Mrs. Smith that her aid would be stopped if she continued her association with Williams—that was the rule. Mrs. Smith protested. She pointed out that Williams was married, his wife worked, they had nine children of their own to care for, and he had never been in a position to help her with more than four or five dollars a month. "Ain't much he can do," she told Mrs. Stancil. "You can't make a man take care of his own kids, much less take care of other people's kids."

Mrs. Smith was angry: her old caseworker and the county's ADC supervisor were called in, and for two hours the three white women attempted to soothe their client. Though she granted that her caseworkers had as a rule been "nice" to her, Mrs. Smith remained critical of Mrs. Stancil: "She didn't have no right to cut my kids off. Sitting down there in that air-conditioned place and saying my kids can't get aid. She never came 'round to my house and found anybody there. I told her, 'As long as I'm not having no more kids for you to support, why should you bother me? You shouldn't be so hard on me.'"

Efforts by Southern states to cleanse their welfare rolls of certain children did not begin with the Smith family. For some years, a number of state welfare departments had a "suitable home" requirement, according to which evidence of a parent's "casual relationships either in or outside the home" might result in a child's being deprived of welfare payments. The U.S. Department of Health, Education, and Welfare ruled that the "suitable home" requirement violated the intent of the Aid to Dependent Children program.

Federal officials suspected that some states were using such provisions in an effort to rid their welfare rolls of blacks. ADC was the only one of Alabama's major assistance programs that had more blacks in it than whites. A study made in the early 1960's showed that 31,057 of the legitimate children receiving aid were black and 21,623 were white; in the illegitimate category, there were 16 black children for every white one. To an Alabama welfare official intent on lopping off a lot of black recipients quickly, ADC was the place to start lopping.

Soon after taking office as commissioner of Alabama's Department of Pensions and Security in January 1963, Ruben K. King set to work on the ADC problem. "I wanted to get down to the real meat of the coconut," said the commissioner, a short and remarkably round man who was appointed by Governor George C. Wallace, although he had never had any training in social work.

In June 1964 Alabama put into effect its substitute-father regulation. Under the rule, an able-bodied male was considered a substitute father of all the children in a given household if he lived in the home with the children's mother "for the purpose of cohabitation"; if he didn't live in the house "regularly" but visited "frequently for the purpose of cohabiting" with the mother; or if he met the mother elsewhere for that purpose. In Alabama, a man could be judged a "substitute father" without ever laying eyes on his substitute children.

The regulation worked. Between 1964 and 1966 some 15,000 children were removed from the relief rolls of Alabama, and applications for aid on behalf of 6,400 children were rejected. What color children? In thirty months, in seven representative counties, 498 cases were closed; 97 per cent of the children were black.

Had Mrs. Smith wished to become eligible again after being barred from aid, she would have had to inform the state that she had broken off with the phantom father and she would have had to have this report corroborated by at least two "acceptable references in a position to know." Singled out as persons in a position to know were law-enforcement officials, ministers, neighbors, grocers. With Mrs. Smith's permission, an investigator would have gone to a policeman or to her grocer to inquire about her relationship with William E. Williams. Mrs. Smith did not grant her caseworker such permission—"I told her it was none of her business."

At no time during her run-in with the Department of Pensions and Security did Mrs. Smith show any of the apathy once associated with welfare recipients. She tended to be high-spirited, generally good-humored, and often jolly, but she was indignant at the idea that the welfare people could punish her family, which she had kept together for years mainly by her own determination and hard work, because they didn't approve of her private doings.

In the fall of 1966 she took her story to some civil-rights workers who had won a reputation around Selma for talking tough to welfare-department officials. From Selma the details were relayed to New York, where the case attracted the attention of a thirty-two-year-old trial lawyer named Martin Garbus, then co-director of the Center on Social Welfare Policy, which had recently been organized to test the nation's welfare laws.

In November 1966 Garbus filed an action in Mrs. Smith's behalf in Federal District Court in Montgomery. He asked that the suit be heard by a three-judge federal court which could rule on the constitutional issues. This was granted—and the case was on its way to the Supreme Court.

At this point, we may bid goodbye to Mrs. Smith, for the case in truth was no longer hers. It had become a "class action"—brought in behalf of "all other persons similarly situated," the tens of thousands of mothers and hundreds of thousands of children who were being deprived of aid by the substitute-father rules of nineteen states and the District of Columbia. Mrs. Smith had provided the legal wedge. With the doors of the courtroom now open, she was transformed into "Mrs. Sylvester Smith, *et al.*, plaintiffs."

The case moved with remarkable speed. In November 1967, just a year after the original complaint, a three-judge U.S. court delivered its decision. The judges called the substitute-father rule "arbitrary and discriminatory" and declared that it violated the Equal Protection Clause of the Fourteenth Amendment by permitting Alabama to "pick and choose the mothers and children it will aid through the use of some classifications which are not rationally related to the purpose of the applicable statutes."

The State of Alabama appealed. The Supreme Court had not previously entered the tangled area of public welfare, but there was a feeling in the air that it was ready to do so—indeed, eager for the opportunity. The times demanded it; the case invited it; and, after all, it was natural for a Court identified with civil rights to move from school and voting cases to welfare.*

Boyish-looking attorney Garbus had never argued a case before the high Court, but he had a quick mind and a tongue to keep up with it. He took pains to prepare himself for each Justice's probable approach to welfare programs. Justice Fortas, for example, wanted to know what prevented the federal Department of Health, Education, and Welfare from simply ruling out unacceptable state programs. Garbus explained that HEW's sole power was to withhold funds altogether—a drastic penalty which federal officials were loath to

---

* *King, Commissioner, Department of Pensions & Security* et al. v. *Smith* et al., 392 U.S. 309 (1968).

apply. Justice Harlan, reflecting the attitudes of Justices White and Stewart, questioned the right of the federal government to set up standards for a state program; he was surprised to learn that 83 per cent of Alabama's ADC funds were contributed by Washington.

The *Smith* case was argued not long after the assassination of Martin Luther King, Jr., and as the lawyers and judges discussed what a Southern state had done to thousands of its poorest families, a level of emotion was reached not customary in the Supreme Court building. In his replies to the friendly questions of Justice Brennan, Garbus emphasized that the class being discriminated against was composed of "helpless children." When the Assistant Attorney General of Alabama argued that in cutting off aid to mothers having illicit relationships, her state was providing more money for qualifying families, Justice Brennan commented tartly: "You give more milk to some children by giving none to others." And after a series of evasive responses by the Alabama attorney regarding the circumstances under which a family could be deprived of aid, Chief Justice Warren ended the hearing by saying: "Never mind! Never mind!" and slammed a book down on his desk.

The Justices seemed to be searching for a decision that would be phrased in the narrowest terms yet have the widest application. The way to achieve this, suggested Garbus, was for the Court to hold that states may treat as "parents," for purposes of ADC eligibility, only persons with a legal obligation to support the children—

that is, their real fathers or their mothers' husbands. Friends of the mother like William E. Williams would not fall into this category, and so their presence could not be used to deprive children of state aid.

That is the line the Court took. To the Justices, it seemed "inconceivable" that Alabama was free to discourage immorality by disqualifying needy children from aid. The Social Security Act stated that aid was to be granted to all eligible children, and, they ruled, so it must be.

Chief Justice Warren, in the name of a unanimous Court, wrote: "We hold today only that Congress has made at least this one determination: that destitute children who are legally fatherless cannot be flatly denied federally funded assistance on the transparent fiction that they have a substitute father." Justice Warren had already made known his intention to retire, and Martin Garbus said: "I like to think that Warren purposely saved the *Smith* case for his final opinion."

The great issue at the center of the *Smith* case and cases still to come is whether individuals are diminished in the eyes of the law because they are poor and need help. Attorney Garbus saw his victory as the beginning of a full-scale attack on a whole array of state welfare practices: "The era of school and voting litigation is giving way to the era of poverty litigation. With the *Smith* case, the courts have established that the Federal Government has the final say as to the purpose of Federal welfare programs. This is the beginning of a new welfare bill of rights."

King v. Smith
1968

BLACK	Concurred
REED	
FRANKFURTER	
DOUGLAS	Concurring opinion
JACKSON	
BURTON	
CLARK	
MINTON	
WARREN	OPINION OF COURT
HARLAN	Concurred
BRENNAN	Concurred
WHITTAKER	
STEWART	Concurred
WHITE	Concurred
GOLDBERG	
FORTAS	Concurred
MARSHALL	Concurred

CASES CITED

I | SEPARATE AND UNEQUAL

Brown et al. *v. Board of Education of Topeka* et al., 347 U.S. 483 (1954)
Plessy v. Ferguson, 163 U.S. 537 (1896)
Cooper et al., *Members of the Board of Directors of the Little Rock, Arkansas, Independent School District* et al. *v. Aaron* et al., 358 U.S. 1 (1958)
Griffin et al. *v. County School Board of Prince Edward County* et al., 377 U.S. 218 (1964)
Heart of Atlanta Motel v. United States et al., 379 U.S. 241 (1964)
Richard Perry Loving et ux. *v. Virginia,* 388 U.S. 1 (1967)
Harper et al. *v. Virginia Board of Elections* et al., 383 U.S. 663 (1966)

II | THE WALL BETWEEN CHURCH AND STATE

Illinois ex Rel. McCollum v. Board of Education, 333 U.S. 203 (1948)
Zorach v. Clauson, 343 U.S. 306 (1952)
Engel et al. *v. Vitale* et al., 370 U.S. 421 (1962)
School District of Abington Township, Pennsylvania, et al. *v. Schempp* et al.; *Murray* et al. *v. Curlett* et al., *Con-*

stituting the Board of School Commissioners of Baltimore City, 374 U.S. 203 (1963)

III | THE RIGHTS OF SUSPECTED CRIMINALS

Betts v. Brady, 316 U.S. 455 (1942)
Gideon v. Wainwright, Corrections Director, 372 U.S. 335 (1963)
Escobedo v. Illinois, 378 U.S. 478 (1964)
Miranda v. Arizona, 384 U.S. 436 (1966)

IV | THE YOUNG HAVE RIGHTS, TOO

In re Gault, 387 U.S. 1 (1967)

V | THE ZONE OF PRIVACY

Griswold et al. *v. Connecticut,* 381 U.S. 479 (1965)

VI | THE END OF CENSORSHIP

Roth v. United States; Alberts v. California, 354 U.S. 476 (1957)
Jacobellis v. Ohio, 378 U.S. 184 (1964)
A Book Named "John Cleland's Memoirs of a Woman of Pleasure" et al. *v. Attorney General of Massachusetts,* 383 U.S. 413 (1966)
Mishkin v. New York, 383 U.S. 502 (1966)
Ginzburg v. United States, 383 U.S. 463 (1966)

VII | THE RIGHT TO BE UNPOPULAR

Adler v. Board of Education, 342 U.S. 485 (1952)
Elfbrandt v. Russell et al., 384 U.S. 11 (1966)
Keyishian et al. *v. Board of Regents of the University of the State of New York* et al., 385 U.S. 589 (1967)
Aptheker et al. *v. Secretary of State,* 378 U.S. 500 (1964)

CASES CITED

VIII | ONE MAN—ONE VOTE

Colegrove et al. *v. Green* et al., 328 U.S. 549 (1946)
Baker et al. *v. Carr* et al., 369 U.S. 186 (1962)
Gray, Chairman of the Georgia State Democratic Executive Committee, et al. *v. Sanders,* 372 U.S. 368 (1963)
Wesberry et al. *v. Sanders, Governor of Georgia,* et al., 376 U.S. 1 (1964)
Reynolds, Judge, et al. *v. Sims* et al., 377 U.S. 533 (1964)

IX | MILK FOR CHILDREN

King, Commissioner, Department of Pensions & Security, et al. *v. Smith* et al., 392 U.S. 309 (1968)

JUSTICES WHO SERVED ON THE WARREN COURT, 1953–1969

Hugo L. Black*   1937–
Stanley F. Reed   1938–1957
Felix Frankfurter   1939–1962
William O. Douglas*   1939–
Robert H. Jackson   1941–1954
Harold H. Burton   1945–1958
Tom C. Clark   1949–1967
Sherman Minton   1949–1956
Earl Warren   1953–1969
John M. Harlan*   1955–
William J. Brennan, Jr.*   1956–
Charles E. Whittaker   1957–1962
Potter Stewart*   1958–
Byron R. White*   1962–
Arthur J. Goldberg   1962–1965
Abe Fortas   1965–1969
Thurgood Marshall*   1967–

* Currently on the Court.

HUGO L. BLACK was named to the Supreme Court by President Franklin D. Roosevelt in 1937. Black was born in Harlan, Alabama, on February 27, 1886. Both his parents died while he was a child, and he was raised by an older brother. As a boy, he became fascinated with the goings on at the local courthouse and decided at an early age that he wanted to be a lawyer. He worked his way through the University of Alabama, where he was awarded a law degree in 1906. With $1.20 as capital, he began to practice law in Ashland, Alabama. He was a county prosecutor for two years and then, after duty in World War I, he returned to law practice and politics in Birmingham. In 1926 he was elected Senator from Alabama. Although he came to the Senate with a reputation as a Southern conservative, backed by the Ku Klux Klan, he became an ardent proponent of New Deal measures, such as the bill to establish a minimum wage and maximum working hours. He also led a number of notable investigations while in the Senate and was a severe critic of the Supreme Court Justices for their decisions against New Deal projects. His nomination to the high Court brought a barrage of criticism from opponents of the Roosevelt Administration, who charged it was a political appointment and that Black had no judicial experience except for eighteen months as a police judge many years before. In recent years, Black has parted from his liberal colleagues to uphold police actions in cases involving questionable searches, but his long career on the Court has been marked by dedication to civil rights and civil liberties.

STANLEY F. REED served on the Supreme Court from 1938 to 1957. Reed was born on December 31, 1884, in the town of Maysville, Kentucky, where his ancestors had settled in Colonial times. He attended Kentucky Wesleyan College and was a prize-winning student at Yale Law School.

He practiced law in his home town for twenty-five years before coming to Washington, D.C., in 1929 to be general counsel of the Federal Farm Board. In 1932 he moved to the recently created Reconstruction Finance Corporation. And in 1935 he became U.S. Solicitor General, in which role he argued many of the New Deal's cases before the Supreme Court. Appointed to the Court by President Roosevelt in 1938, he took a generally conservative position, showing reluctance to upset the government's administrative procedures and executive regulations when they came into conflict with individuals. His strong point was banking and finance, and he wrote scores of decisions in complicated financial cases during his nineteen years on the bench. Asked in 1957 why he was retiring, this quiet man said simply, "Because I am seventy-two years old."

FELIX FRANKFURTER served on the Supreme Court from 1939 to 1962. Frankfurter was born in Vienna, Austria, on November 15, 1882, and was brought to this country by his parents at the age of twelve. He was among the most illustrious graduates of the City College of New York and went from there to Harvard Law School. In the early 1900's he served in various government posts, and in 1914 he joined the faculty of his alma mater, the Harvard Law School. During the next twenty years, this short, rather dapper man, known for his pince-nez, his peppery wit, his exuberance, and his courageously liberal positions, earned a reputation as one of America's outstanding legal scholars and teachers. In his twenty-three years on the high bench, Frankfurter became the most forceful spokesman for the philosophy of "judicial restraint"—the view that the Court should be very careful about exercising its powers in areas which have not been clearly marked out by the Constitution or by judicial precedent. He retired from the bench in 1962 for reasons of health, and died on February 22, 1965. It is generally agreed that Justice Frankfurter was one of the truly brilliant jurists of his age.

WILLIAM O. DOUGLAS was named to the Supreme Court by President Franklin D. Roosevelt in 1939. Douglas was born in Maine, Minnesota, on October 16, 1898, and was reared in the state of Washington. In his youth, William worked as newsboy, farm hand, junk dealer, janitor, and tutor. He attended Whitman College, in Walla Walla, Washington, where, among other jobs, he washed the clothes of fellow students to support himself. After serving as a buck private in World War I, he worked his way east, with six dollars in his pocket, to study at Columbia Law School; he was graduated second in his class. He taught law at Columbia and at Yale before going to Washington, D.C., to direct an investigation for the Securities and Exchange Commission. He was named chairman of the SEC in 1936 and soon became known for his determination to achieve scrupulous honesty in stock-market transactions, an effort that aroused the wrath of Wall Street. He said at the time: "I've been tagged a 'wild-eyed radical.' Actually, I'm a conservative of the old school. I am the kind of conservative who can't get away from the idea that simple honesty ought to prevail in the financial world." From the SEC, Douglas moved to the Supreme Court at the age of forty-one. In private life he is known as an avid traveler, hiker, and conservationist, as well as a prolific and controversial writer. On the Court he has stood consistently for the enlargement of individual rights, which has been such an important theme in the life of the Warren Court.

ROBERT H. JACKSON served on the Supreme Court from 1941 until his death in 1954. Jackson was born on a farm in Spring Creek, Pennsylvania, on February 13, 1892. Although he was destined to achieve world-wide recognition as a prosecutor and jurist, he never actually got a law degree. He completed two years of work in a single year at Albany Law School, but he was denied his degree because two years of attendance was required. He was admitted to the New York State bar in 1913, at the age of twenty-one, and set up practice in Jamestown, where he became corporation counsel. The state's Governor, Franklin D. Roosevelt, heard of him and appointed him to study and reform New York's judicial system. In 1934, Roosevelt, now President, brought Jackson to Washington to work in a variety of government departments. In 1938 he replaced Stanley Reed as U.S. Solicitor General; of the forty-four cases he argued before the Supreme Court on the government's behalf, he lost only six. In 1940 Jackson became U.S. Attorney General, and the next year he was named to the high Court. After World War II, Justice Jackson achieved special distinction when he was appointed by President Truman as chief U.S. prosecutor in the international war-crimes trial of the top Nazi leaders. (Ten of them went to the gallows; seven received prison sentences; three were acquitted.) "No longer," said Justice Jackson, "may the head of a State consider himself outside the law, and impose inhuman acts on the peoples of the world." Jackson was known for his vigorous and cogent dissents during his years as a Justice, but on May 17, 1954, when the Court outlawed segregation in the public schools, he took his place on the bench despite illness in order to leave no doubt that the Justices were unanimous on this subject.

HAROLD H. BURTON served on the Supreme Court from 1945 to 1958. Burton was born in Jamaica Plain, Massachusetts, then a suburb of Boston, on June 22, 1888. He attended Bowdoin College, in Maine, and Harvard Law School. While working for the telephone company in Cleveland as a pothole digger on a summer vacation from college, he found himself attracted by that city, and on his return from infantry duty in World War I, he settled there. In 1935 Burton won election as reform mayor of Cleveland, which was then ridden by crime and depression. He was re-elected twice by record majorities and presided over the reorganization of the city government. In 1940 he was elected to the Senate from Ohio, and it was from this position that he was named to the Supreme Court by President Harry S Truman. A soft-spoken man, Burton took a central position on the Court. He said, when he was appointed, "I hold to the belief that if folks get around a table and talk things through, they can usually come to the right and fair answer." He retired in 1958, at the age of seventy, and died on October 24, 1964.

TOM C. CLARK served on the Supreme Court from 1949 to 1967. Clark was born in Dallas, Texas, on September 23, 1899. He attended Virginia Military Institute and got his law degree at the University of Texas. He practiced law in his home state until 1937, when he joined the U.S. Department of Justice, rising, in 1943, to the post of Assistant Attorney General in charge of the Antitrust Division. In 1945 he was appointed U.S. Attorney General by President Truman, and the President named him to the Supreme Court. Clark had a reputation for conservative views when appointed, and he took a conservative line as a Justice. He resigned in 1967, when his son Ramsey was nominated to be U.S. Attorney General—and thus a party to many of the cases which come before the Court each year. By resigning, Justice Clark avoided any appearance of impropriety. (In 1930 Charles Evans Hughes, Jr., resigned as U.S. Solicitor General when his father was appointed Chief Justice—a reverse example of the same principle.)

JUSTICES WHO SERVED ON THE WARREN COURT

SHERMAN MINTON served on the Supreme Court from 1949 to 1956. Minton was born in Georgetown, Indiana, on October 20, 1890. At New Albany high school he was a football, baseball, track, and debating star. He graduated at the head of his class from Indiana University and won a scholarship to Yale Law School. After serving in France in World War I, he settled down to the practice of law and Democratic politics in New Albany. He built up a state-wide reputation which brought him election in 1934 as Senator from Indiana. During his one term in the Senate, he acted as a staunch advocate of New Deal measures. At the desk beside him was another young freshman, Harry S Truman; they developed a close friendship. In 1940 Minton lost his Senate seat to a Republican, and in the following year he was appointed to the U.S. Court of Appeals by President Roosevelt. In 1949 President Truman named his old friend "Shay" Minton to the Supreme Court, where he turned out to be much less liberal than during his New Deal days, taking a middle-of-the-road approach to issues. He retired for reasons of health in 1956, and died on April 9, 1965.

EARL WARREN was named Chief Justice of the Supreme Court by President Dwight D. Eisenhower in 1953. Warren was born in Los Angeles, California, on March 19, 1891. His father was a railroad mechanic who had come to this country from Norway; his mother was from a Swedish immigrant family. (The name "Warren" had been changed from Varran by Earl's grandfather.) Young Warren worked his way through the University of California and its law school, from which he graduated in 1914, and took a job with a San Francisco law firm. He was drafted into the Army when the United States entered World War I. After his discharge with the rank of lieutenant, he served as city attorney for Oakland, California, and deputy district attorney for Alameda County. In 1925 he was elected district attorney of Alameda County, and he went on to win two other high elective offices as a Republican—Attorney General of California in 1938 and Governor from 1943 to 1953. Exceedingly popular in his home state, Warren ran for Vice President on the losing Republican ticket with Thomas E. Dewey in 1948, and was a leading contender for the GOP Presidential nomination in 1952. Although he had no judicial experience when he was appointed Chief Justice (becoming the first Californian ever to sit on the high bench), he brought with him a reputation for fairness, moderation, and nonpartisanship. On the Court, which soon became identified with his name, he proved himself to be a wholehearted champion of individual rights. He served for sixteen years, resigning in 1969.

JOHN M. HARLAN was appointed to the Supreme Court by President Eisenhower in 1955. Harlan was born in Chicago, Illinois, on May 20, 1899, the grandson and namesake of Justice John Marshall Harlan, who served on the Court from 1877 to 1911. Young Harlan attended Princeton University and spent three years at Oxford University as a Rhodes Scholar before returning to law school in New York. After graduation he served as an Assistant U.S. Attorney and a Special Assistant Attorney General. He joined a prestigious New York law firm in the early 1930's and built a highly successful career as a trial lawyer, representing such major companies as DuPont. In 1954 he was named to the U.S. Court of Appeals, and on the death of Justice Jackson less than a year later, he reached the high bench. He was often to be found on the dissenting side during the life of the Warren Court. With the retirement of Justice Frankfurter, Harlan's became the main voice warning his colleagues against moving into areas which are not clearly marked out by the Constitution. His opinions are distinguished by their close analyses of the letter of the law.

JUSTICES WHO SERVED ON THE WARREN COURT

WILLIAM J. BRENNAN, JR., was appointed to the Supreme Court by President Eisenhower in 1956. Brennan was born in Newark, New Jersey, on April 25, 1906, one of eight children. His father had come to this country from Ireland in 1890 and worked as a coal shoveler in a brewery and a metal polisher before getting involved in local politics. He went on to serve on the Newark City Commission and as the city's Director of Public Safety. As a child, William worked at odd jobs: he delivered milk, helped out in a filling station, made change for passengers waiting for trolley cars. At school he won so many prizes that a former classmate complained, "There was none left for the rest of us." He attended the University of Pennsylvania and got his law degree from Harvard Law School in 1931. He practiced law in Newark for nearly twenty years—with time out for service as an officer in World War II. In 1949 he was appointed to the New Jersey Superior Court; in 1952 he was named to the state Supreme Court. A friend described him as "the friendly Irish type—very convivial, easy-going. A great storyteller." At the age of fifty, on the retirement of Justice Minton, Brennan took his seat on the U.S. Supreme Court, where he has voted with the liberal wing.

CHARLES E. WHITTAKER served on the Supreme Court from 1957 to 1962. Whittaker was born in Troy, Kansas, on February 22, 1901. He worked afternoons as an office boy for a law firm in Kansas City, Missouri, while attending law school at the University of Kansas City. Admitted to the Missouri bar in 1923, he became a leading lawyer in that state. In 1954 he was named a federal district judge by President Eisenhower, and he was promoted to the Circuit Court of Appeals in 1956. The following year, on the retirement of Justice Reed, the President appointed him to the high Court, where he was the only Justice from his section of the country. During his five years on the Court, he tended to vote with the conservative wing. In cases involving Communists, for example, it seemed to him that individual liberty was outweighed by the needs of the government. He was a modest man who admitted that he felt oppressed by the burden of his responsibilities—the large amount of reading required of him, and the difficulty and importance of the issues he was called upon to decide. This pressure played a part in his retirement from the Court in 1962, on the advice of his physician.

POTTER STEWART was appointed to the Supreme Court by President Eisenhower in 1958. Stewart was born in Jackson, Michigan, on January 23, 1915. He grew up in Cincinnati, Ohio, the son of a lawyer who became Mayor of Cincinnati and later was a justice of the Ohio Supreme Court. After graduating with honors from Yale University, young Stewart studied for a year at Cambridge University in England, then returned to Yale Law School. He practiced law successfully in New York and Cincinnati, where he served on the city council. As a partner in a Cincinnati law firm, he represented such giant companies as Procter & Gamble before being appointed to the U.S. Court of Appeals in 1954. Asked at the time whether he felt suited for the post despite a lack of judicial experience, he said, "Being fair-minded is something that's either there or not." His record on the Court of Appeals led to his being selected in 1958, at the age of forty-three, to fill the seat of Justice Burton. Stewart has tended to take a relatively conservative position, notably in cases involving the rights of defendants in criminal cases.

BYRON R. WHITE was named to the Supreme Court by President John F. Kennedy in 1962. White was born in Fort Collins, Colorado, on June 8, 1917, and grew up in Wellington, a small town near the Wyoming border. At the University of Colorado, where the 6' 2" scholar-athlete earned the nickname "Whizzer" for his abilities as an All-America halfback, he got straight A's—except for two courses in which he received B's. He played professional football to finance his studies at Yale Law School—and became the best-paid football player of his day. He gave up this lucrative career after graduation to accept the highly valued post of law clerk to Chief Justice Fred Vinson. While a Rhodes scholar at Oxford University in 1939, he met John F. Kennedy, son of the then U.S. Ambassador to Great Britain. They met again in the Pacific during the war, when both were naval officers, and the relationship developed in Washington after the war. In the 1960 Democratic primaries, White headed the Kennedy campaign in Colorado, and during the Presidential elections he was chairman of the nationwide Citizens for Kennedy organization. Attorney General Robert F. Kennedy selected White as his Deputy Attorney General, in which post he won a reputation for quiet efficiency. On his appointment to the high bench at the age of forty-four, to replace Justice Whittaker, it was widely assumed that he would join the liberal wing, but, as it turned out, he has been found more often than not on the conservative side in split decisions.

ARTHUR J. GOLDBERG served on the Supreme Court from 1962 to 1965. Goldberg was born in Chicago, Illinois, on August 8, 1908, the last of eleven children of Russian immigrants. His father was a peddler who moved with his family from San Francisco to Texas and finally to Chicago, where he made his living by carting fruits and vegetables to the city's markets and hotels. Arthur grew up in a rough neighborhood, where fights were not always settled by judicial means. While attending Northwestern Law School, he earned twenty dollars a week by writing briefs for a Chicago law firm. Graduating at the top of his class, he went into labor law. His career was interrupted by service as an Army officer in World War II. From 1948 to 1961 he held the position of general counsel to the CIO and, after the merger of the nation's major labor unions, to the AFL–CIO. President Kennedy appointed Goldberg Secretary of Labor in 1961, and from there he was named to the Supreme Court, to replace Justice Frankfurter, in what some thought of as the Court's "Jewish seat." During his brief tenure, he was identified with the Court's liberal wing. He resigned in 1965, at the urging of President Lyndon B. Johnson, to take the post of U.S. Representative to the United Nations, which he held until 1968. In 1970 he ran unsuccessfully on the Democratic ticket for Governor of New York.

ABE FORTAS served on the Supreme Court from 1965 to 1969. He was born in Memphis, Tennessee, on June 19, 1910, the son of a Jewish cabinetmaker who had come to this country from England. In his youth, Abe earned cash by playing the violin at social gatherings; his love for the instrument would stay with him throughout his life. He chalked up a brilliant record at Yale Law School, where he studied under then Professor William O. Douglas. Going to Washington early in the New Deal years, Fortas, not yet thirty, rose to be Under Secretary of the Interior. In the 1940's he became a highly influential Washington lawyer and won a reputation for assisting the powerless as well as the powerful—juvenile offenders, penniless suspects, and alleged security risks. He also won a reputation for intellectual arrogance. He was appointed to the high bench by President Johnson, to whom he had been an intimate adviser for nearly twenty years, and took Justice Goldberg's place with the Warren Court's liberal majority. In 1968, after Earl Warren made known his intention to retire, the President nominated Abe Fortas to be Chief Justice. The nomination met strong resistance from a conservative bloc in the Senate and had to be withdrawn. A year later, Justice Fortas resigned amid charges that he had accepted a $20,000 fee from a businessman while serving on the Court. It was generally agreed that the Court thus lost an unusually astute legal mind.

THURGOOD MARSHALL was named to the Supreme Court in 1967 by President Johnson, the first black man ever to sit on the high bench. Marshall was born in Baltimore, Maryland, on July 2, 1908, the son of a Pullman-car steward and the great-grandson of a slave. His parents sacrificed to help him through college—his mother selling her engagement ring to pay part of his expenses—and in 1933 he was graduated at the top of his class from Howard University Law School. In 1938 he became head of the legal staff of the National Association for the Advancement of Colored People (NAACP), and for the next twenty-three years he was the foremost advocate in the courts of black Americans' efforts to gain their full rights under the Constitution. Of the thirty-two cases he argued before the Supreme Court, his most notable victory came in the 1954 decision outlawing segregation in the schools. He was appointed a judge of the U.S. Court of Appeals by President Kennedy in 1961. In the summer of 1965 he was named U.S. Solicitor General, the federal official responsible for deciding which cases the government should take to the Supreme Court and who should argue them. He held this post until his appointment to the high Court to replace Justice Clark. President Johnson said of the appointment: "I believe it is the right thing to do, the right time to do it, the right man, and the right place." On the Warren Court, Justice Marshall has voted with the liberal wing, showing the same feeling for the human impact of the law that had marked his career as a lawyer.

INDEX

Abington School District v. Schempp, 53, 59, 163
Adler v. Board of Education, 125, 132, 164
Aid to Dependent Children, 151–60
Alabama Dept. of Pensions and Security, 155–6
Alberts v. California, 108, 164
American Civil Liberties Union, 45, 51, 86
American Ethical Union, 46
American Jewish Committee, 46
Aptheker, Herbert, 130–1

Aptheker v. Secretary of State, 129, 133, 164
Arkansas General Assembly, 24
Atlanta Constitution, 22

Baker v. Carr, 138, 148, 165
Betts, Smith, 63
Betts v. Brady, 64, 80, 164
Black, Hugo L., 29, 36, 40, 42–3, 46–7, 58, 64–5, 76 n., 80, 89–91, 99, 101–2, 105, 110, 115–17, 120, 126, 131–2, 137, 141–2, 148, 161, 167–8
Blackmun, Harry A., 76 n.

INDEX

Brandeis, Louis D., 144
Brennan, William J., Jr., 36, 54–5, 58, 76 n., 80, 91, 105, 108–9, 112, 115–16, 120, 128–9, 132, 138, 148, 159, 161, 167, 175
Brown, Henry B., 17
Brown, Linda Carol, 15–16, 19, 21–2, 34, 152
Brown, Oliver, 15–16
Brown v. Board of Education, 7, 19–21, 23, 27–8, 30, 34, 36, 163
Burger, Warren E., 76 n.
Burton, Harold H., 36, 58, 80, 91, 105, 120, 132, 148, 161, 167, 171–2, 176
Buxton, C. Lee, 94–6, 98, 100, 103
Byrnes, James F., 80 n.

California State Senate, 136, 145
Clark, Ramsey, 78, 172
Clark, Tom C., 31, 36, 54, 58, 70, 75, 80, 91, 105, 114, 120, 128, 131–2, 139, 143, 148, 161, 167, 172
Cleland, John, 114
Colegrove v. Green, 137, 148, 165
Columbia University Law School, 84

Communist Party, 124, 129–31
Comstock, Anthony, 95
Connecticut House of Representatives, 136
Cooper v. Aaron, 26, 36, 163

Department of Health, Education, and Welfare, 155, 158
Department of State, 129
Dewey, Thomas E., 174
Douglas, William O., 31, 33, 36, 42, 47, 55, 58, 64, 76 n., 80, 91, 99–100, 105, 110–11, 114–16, 120, 126–7, 129–30, 132, 137, 140, 148, 161, 167, 170, 178

Eisenhower, Dwight D., 3, 20, 25, 48, 173–6
Elfbrandt, Barbara, 126–7
Elfbrandt, Vernon, 126–7
Elfbrandt v. Russell, 127–8, 133, 164
Engel, Stephen, 46
Engel v. Vitale, 46, 59, 163
Escobedo, Danny, 67–9, 72, 76, 78
Escobedo v. Illinois, 69–70, 75–6, 81, 164

Fanny Hill, 114–15
Faubus, Orval E., 24, 152

181

INDEX

Federal Bureau of Investigation, 68
Feinberg Law, 124–8
Flynn, Elizabeth Gurley, 129, 131
Fortas, Abe, 36, 58, 65, 80, 83, 87–8, 91, 105, 120, 132, 148, 158, 161, 167, 178–9
Frankfurter, Felix, 24–6, 36, 43, 58, 80, 91, 105, 120, 132, 137–40, 148, 161, 167, 169–70, 174, 178
Fuller, Louis, 153

Garbus, Martin, 157–60
Gault, Gerald Francis, 85–8, 90
Gideon, Clarence Earl, 62–6, 152
Gideon v. Wainwright, 65, 67, 70, 81, 614
Ginzburg, Ralph, 116, 118
Ginzburg v. U.S., 115–16, 121, 164
Goldberg, Arthur J., 36, 54–5, 58, 69–70, 80, 91, 101–2, 105, 112, 120, 130–2, 148, 161, 167, 177–8
Graham, Billy, 48
Gray v. Sanders, 140, 149, 165
Griffin v. County School Board, 29, 36, 163

Griswold, Estelle, 94–5, 98, 100
Griswold v. Connecticut, 98, 103, 105, 164

Harlan, John Marshall, 36, 55, 58, 70–1, 75–6, 80, 89, 91, 105, 116–17, 120, 128, 131–2, 138–40, 142–3, 148, 159, 161, 167, 174
Harlan, John Marshall (1833–1911), 18–19, 174
Harper v. Virginia Board of Elections, 33, 37, 163
Heart of Atlanta Motel v. U.S., 31, 37, 163
Hoover, Herbert, 48
Hughes, Charles Evans, Jr., 172

In re Gault, 86–7, 91, 164

Jackson, Robert H., 36, 43–4, 58, 80, 91, 105, 120, 132, 148, 161, 167, 170–1, 174
Jacobellis v. Ohio, 112, 120, 164
Johnson, Lyndon B., 178–9

Kennedy, John F., 28, 48, 176–9

182

INDEX

Kennedy, Robert F., 146, 177
Keyishian v. Board of Regents, 128, 133, 164
King James Bible, 48
King, Martin Luther, Jr., 159
King, Ruben K., 155
King v. Smith, 152, 158–61, 165
Ku Klux Klan, 168

Lewis, Anthony, 66
Lincoln, Abraham, 141
Little Rock School Board, 24–6
Lord's Prayer, 51, 52
Lovers, The, 112–14
Loving, Richard P., 32
Loving v. Virginia, 32, 37, 163

McCollum v. Board of Education, 42, 58, 163
Madison, James, 40
Marshall, Thurgood, 19–20, 36, 58, 76 n., 80, 91, 105, 120, 132, 148, 161, 167, 179
"Memoirs" v. Attorney General, 114, 121, 164
Minton, Sherman, 36, 58, 80, 91, 105, 120, 125, 132, 148, 161, 167, 173, 175
Miranda, Ernesto Arthur, 72, 75–6

Miranda v. Arizona, 72, 76–8, 81, 164
Mishkin v. New York, 115, 121, 164
Murphy, Frank, 58 n., 80 n., 137, 148 n.
Murray, Madalyn, 53, 55–7
Murray, William J., 52, 57
Murray v. Curlett, 53

NAACP, 19–20, 179
National Council of Catholic Men, 97
National Council of Churches, 49
New Republic, 116
New York State Board of Regents, 44, 124, 128
New York Times, 66

Planned Parenthood, 94, 98
Plessy, Homer Adolph, 17
Plessy v. Ferguson, 16, 18, 33, 163
Political Affairs, 130

Reader's Digest, 77
Reed, Stanley F., 36, 58, 80, 91, 105, 120, 132, 148, 161, 167–8, 171, 175
Reynolds v. Sims, 143, 149, 165
Roberts, Owen J., 64, 80 n.
Roman Catholic Church, 47–8, 96

183

INDEX

Roosevelt, Franklin D., 168–71, 173
Roth, Lawrence, 45, 50–1
Roth v. U.S., 108, 112, 120, 164
Russell, Richard B., 146
Rutledge, Wiley, 58 n., 148 n.

Schempp, Ellory, 51–2
Smith, Ernestine, 153
Smith, Ida Elizabeth, 153
Smith, Mrs. Sylvester, 151–7
Smith, Willie James, 153
Smith, Willie Lewis, 153
Stancil, Jacquelyn, 154
State University of New York, 127
Stewart, Potter, 36, 46–7, 54, 58, 70–1, 75, 76 n., 80, 89, 91, 98–9, 101, 105, 115–17, 120, 128, 132, 143, 148, 159, 161, 167, 176
Stone, Harlan F., 80 n., 148 n.
Sumner Elementary School, 16
Synagogue Council of America, 46

Talmadge, Herman, 22
Truman, Harry S, 171–3

University of Buffalo, 127

Vinson, Frederick M., 58–9 n., 132 n., 177
Vitale, William J., Jr., 46

Wallace, George C., 155
Warren, Earl, 3, 5, 20–1, 32, 36, 41, 58, 72–4, 80, 91, 105, 114, 120, 124, 132, 145, 148, 159–61, 167, 173–4, 178
Wesberry v. Sanders, 141, 143, 149, 165
White, Byron R., 36, 58, 70–1, 75–6, 80, 89, 91, 105, 120, 128, 131–2, 148, 159, 161, 167, 176–7
Whittaker, Charles E., 36, 58, 80, 91, 105, 120, 132, 148, 161, 167, 175–6, 177

Zorach v. Clauson, 42, 59, 163

1/997